# A
# DIFFERENT
# COLLEGE
# EXPERIENCE

The four years I spent at a small Christian university in North Carolina were some of the most formative days of my life. They shaped me and changed me, like they do for anyone who experiences college life. So many lessons learned, so many relationships formed, so many mistakes made. In my opinion, *A Different College Experience* should be required reading for every Christian who feels like college is their next step after high school. But it should be more than required reading, it should be required living. This is a Christ-centered, gospel-oriented book that digs deeper than the typical moral advice of "don't sleep around" and "find a good Bible study group." This book gets to the root issue of your identity, what you believe about God, and how your relationship with Him sets the course for the direction your life will go as you enter college. You don't have to press pause on your faith during this season of your life. Instead, college is the perfect experience to ground yourself in the gospel and learn how to be on mission for the kingdom of God. It's readable, practical, and doable. I wish this book had been written when I was a college student.

**Clayton King**, teaching pastor, Newspring Church, founder and president, Crossroads Camps and Missions, and author of *True Love Project* and *Grounded*

I have spent my entire adult life trying to prepare students to keep their faith as they journey through the "wilderness years" of university and college. One of the greatest challenges is providing outgoing seniors/incoming freshman with a real resource that can have an edifying impact on the trajectory of their journey. In *A Different College Experience* Ben Trueblood and Brian Mills have now provided all of this with that resource! I can't wait to use this breath-of-fresh-air resource to further equip and encourage the amazing young men and women in my ministry at Student Leadership University!

**Brent Crowe**, vice president, Student Leadership University

Honestly, I wish this book would have been written when I was in college. This is NOT a handbook of how to get through college as a Christian, but rather a holistic discipleship worldview during one of the most crucial and formative seasons of a person's life. The emphasis is not on being good or on not being bad, but on having a right view of God, of self, and of the gospel. This book is both theological and practical, and I want to make this required reading for all of my college students.

> **Drew Worsham**, college and young adult pastor,
> Community Bible Church, San Antonio, Texas

I came to know Christ as a senior in high school and the Lord used my college years to deepen my understanding of the gospel, give me a passion for community with other believers, and ignite in me a commitment to the mission of the local church. This is not only my story but the story of many who the Lord has transformed during their college years. By helping readers become rooted in the gospel, their identity in Christ, and God's Word, *A Different College Experience* paves the way for a person's college years to be a time of great spiritual growth. This book is a needed and helpful resource for the church and families during a critical moment of life.

> **Eric Geiger**, senior pastor,
> Mariner's Church, Irvine, California

*A Different College Experience* is a doctrinally rich and incredibly practical book that you'll want to ensure all of your students have read before they are launched to their college and university campuses. Loaded with a passion for the kingdom of God, the local church, and the students you've been investing in, Trueblood and Mills have put together a book that serves as an echoing voice to the hopes, dreams, desires, and hours of investment you've put in to your students since they entered your ministry. It's a must-read.

**Jason Gaston**, family ministries pastor, The Summit Church

BEN TRUEBLOOD & BRIAN MILLS

# A DIFFERENT COLLEGE EXPERIENCE

FOLLOWING CHRIST IN COLLEGE

B&H
PUBLISHING GROUP

NASHVILLE, TENNESSEE

978-1-4627-9424-9

Published by B&H Publishing Group
Nashville, Tennessee

Dewey Decimal Classification: 248.834
Subject Heading: COLLEGE STUDENTS \ CHRISTIAN LIFE \
STUDENTS

2 3 4 5 6 7 8 • 23 22 21 20 19

# Contents

# Preface

I was extremely excited to go to college; however, I was also quite anxious. It was not the coming to college part I was scared of, but the leaving home part. At this time in my life, my family was in shambles. My parents were on the brink of divorce and it seemed as if every relationship in my family was full of tension. You would think I would have been excited to move out, but in reality I felt guilty for leaving and helpless knowing that I would be so far away. I was carrying a burden with me that was way too heavy for my soul to handle. A burden I was not meant to carry.

In the midst of this struggle when I thought I could not handle it anymore, God swooped in and did what only He can do. He carried my burdens and healed me of my hurts. Where I felt like there was nothing more I could do, He showed me that I did not need to do anything but depend on Him: "Fear not, for I am with you; be not dismayed, for I am your God; I will strengthen you, I will help you, I will uphold you with my righteous right hand" (Isa. 41:10 ESV). In the midst of His presence, I found peace in my storm.

Whether you are in a situation like mine or you are battling with your own storm, know that the Lord is good and He is faithful. Through all aspects of college, the Lord will sustain you. If you know this to be truth, living out your faith in college will not be difficult at all. It will be a soul-fulfilling journey and God will use you in unbelievable ways. All you must do to live your best life in college is depend on Him. I promise that anything college has to offer you is incomparable to what God has in store.

Since leaving for school freshman year, I have seen the Lord use me in so many ways, but mainly in regard to my family. It is almost as if He pulled me out of the situation so that I could see it through His eyes. I empathize with you who are reading this and are in a similar situation with the same emotions because I know how bad it hurts. But trust God to be God. He will take care of you and your family and bring you peace. You have the special opportunity to seek God with nothing holding you back, so do it! See how the Lord can move in you and through you in your dorm, classes, sports team, family, and anywhere else He might place you.

—Ashton Childree, Elementary Education major at the University of Arkansas

**THERE IS NOTHING LIKE** the college experience. It's one of those things in life that truly is what you make of it.

We wrote this book because we are passionate about high school and college students. Throughout our time in ministry, we've seen a lot of things go wrong in people's lives because of an incorrect view of the college experience. We want you to succeed in your college years and we believe that it can be the best experience of your life so far, but that will require you to make some difficult choices. You won't be able to approach your college years like most of the people around you.

This book will help you understand more about your faith, or perhaps begin your own faith journey, and will help you to know how to make decisions that are built on the Word of God. When you are done with the next four (or more) years of your life, you should be more equipped than ever to embrace the life God has for you. We want to challenge you to take on that life with great wisdom and discernment.

During your college years you will turn twenty-one, potentially find a spouse, be confronted with the greatest temptation you have ever faced, and will have more freedom than you've ever had. Are you ready? The freshman-year mistakes happen because most are not. Don't let the college experience get the best of you; get the best out of it. This book will help you do so.

# Part 1

# New Beginnings

# Chapter 1

# What Is the Gospel?

College is a challenging, yet rewarding season of life, filled with much change and uncertainty, but rich in new opportunities and growth. My first year of college I questioned the Lord's faithfulness in my life. Had He led me to the right university? Would I ever have Christ-centered friendships? Is it really possible to live out my faith on a campus where many of the students are unchurched and haven't even heard the name of Jesus?

I am three years into my college experience and I have seen the goodness and faithfulness of the Lord in my life particularly in those areas where doubt and uncertainty once flourished. Jesus . . . He really is good, faithful, and trustworthy in all areas of our lives. He writes a more beautiful story than anything you or I could ever write for ourselves. Amidst the Lord's faithfulness, unfortunately there is a thief who wants to steal, kill, and destroy your life and mine. The enemy knows he can use this season of opportunity and growth to steal your hope and kill your dreams.

It is crucial to surround yourself with like-minded people who are running hard after Jesus, who can help keep you accountable in your walk with Christ. Staying spiritually healthy in college is challenging; however, by immersing yourself in godly community and staying in the Word of God, you can be victorious in this season of change. Surrounding myself with Christ-centered community is the best decision I have made during my time in college. This season of life brings much change—new city, new friends, new church, new everything, but you can hold tight to the truth that Jesus never changes, and just as He has shown Himself faithful in my life, He will show Himself faithful in yours.

—Meredith Franzke, junior, University of Arkansas studying Hospitality and Event Planning; Cross Church College small group leader; diamond doll with the University of Arkansas's baseball team


**YOU ARE IN A** unique moment in your life. You've heard that already. You can probably still hear the Dr. Seuss quotes and "one chapter is closing and an exciting new chapter is about to begin" echoing in your head from the graduation speech that already seems like so long ago. You are in a unique moment in your life because, for many of you, you're taking responsibility for your life for the first time. Yes, you have lived with responsibility and consequences (some more than others) before, but to some extent, there has been the covering of parents, other family members, a caring teacher, or a church leader. Now, it is up to you.

The everyday decisions about when you will wake up, what you are going to eat, when you will find time for friends, if you will study, and how often you will wash your clothes now fall to you and you alone. The transition into the college years is a unique moment in your life, not just because you are transitioning schools and perhaps moving to a different place, but you are in a sense experiencing a transfer of ownership over your very own life. It is in this "transfer of ownership" that so many college students make choices that cause them and others incredible pain and baggage.

As a student pastor for many years I have seen students take ownership of their lives and live abundantly, experiencing the college years in a God-honoring, productive, and exciting way. And I have seen the opposite take place, including the life-altering consequences of what our culture would refer to as "the college experience." Which will you choose? It's a lot to take in, I know.

If there is one thing I want you to hear as you begin the journey through this book, it is this: *There is hope*. You can have an incredible college experience and close this next chapter of your life with relationships, memories, education, and a whole lot of fun, while avoiding the land mines that are in front of you. There is hope because of Jesus. There is hope because of what Jesus has done for you, what He can do in you, and what He hopes to do through you. And that is a fitting place to start our journey together here and your journey through the college years.

Dr. Jay Strack is a good friend of mine and is the president of an organization called Student Leadership University. He has spent his life pouring into teenagers and helping grow them into the leaders God has called them to be. A frequent statement I have heard him say applies directly to you at this point in your life: "In everyone's life there is a point where the little boy or girl chooses to sit down and the man or woman chooses to stand up." This is a statement of ownership and responsibility. We've mentioned a few of the everyday life kinds of things that you must now "own," but in no way is it a complete list. Conspicuously absent from that list is the most important piece of your life to take ownership of: your spiritual life.

I know that there are people at various places in their spiritual journey who are sitting with this book right now. Some came to faith as a child, others as a teenager, some are trying to figure out what to do with Jesus, and some are still far from Him. Wherever you are in your spiritual journey, we all have the same starting point: the gospel of Jesus. Your understanding of the gospel is the single greatest influence on what your life will be like during your college years and into the future. So, in your faith, it is time for the little boy or girl to sit down and the man or woman to stand up.

## Hand-Me-Down Faith

Let me shoot straight with you for a second.

If you grew up in church, in a Christian school or home, there's a good chance that you believe what you do about the gospel because it is something your parents, teachers, youth pastor, or other church leaders taught you. It was something they passed on to you, and you believed them.

It's great that these leaders in your life are Christians, but there's a danger here: if I described you just now, there's a good chance that, left on your own, you will be unable to explain why you believe what you do about the gospel. There's a good chance that you are inconsistent at best with time that you spend reading your Bible and praying. And there's a good chance that what you believe about the gospel hasn't translated into specific ways that it shapes who you are and how you live.

Before you angrily close the book, hold on one more second and hear me out. I know there's a good chance for these things to be true because I've seen thousands of students fit this description throughout my time in student ministry. And I've also fit this description myself.

As a high school student in a Christian home, involved in a great church, and at a Christian school, I had a hand-me-down faith. I believed it because other people whom I loved believed. Truth be told, I struggled in my faith, at times doubting my belief, and at other times being sure of it. Once the doubting of faith was settled, my struggle moved on to wondering if I was a good enough Christian, if I was strong enough in my faith. I was a leader in the youth ministry and was at that time the only one of three children "walking with Jesus" in the eyes of my parents. The expectations I felt were like a mountain of burden that lasted through my college years and beyond as I struggled to know if my faith was strong enough, if I was "good enough."

Because of this I often found myself simply trying harder or giving more effort to living a "good Christian life," but at the same time, I found myself on the losing side of my personal battles with sin and temptation. It was like I was constantly running but never going anywhere. This kind of life is painful and exhausting, and is the furthest thing from the abundant life that Jesus said is available to us (John 10:10).

The "good enough" struggle is a real one that plagues many, and it begins in the minds of believers who have not yet taken the step to truly own their faith. They're still living in a hand-me-down Christianity. I was meant for so much more than life on a spiritual treadmill, constantly running and going nowhere. You are too. It's time for you to jump off of the treadmill and take ownership of your faith, which begins with an understanding of the gospel.

## The Gospel

What comes to your mind when you hear the word *gospel*? Literally, it means "good news." So, the gospel of Jesus is literally the good news of Jesus.

J. D. Greear, in his book *Gospel*, defines it this way: "The gospel is the announcement that God has reconciled us to Himself by sending His Son Jesus to die as a substitute for our sins, and that all who repent and believe have eternal life in Him."[1] It may be the case that you've heard something like this before. If so, don't move on from here thinking there isn't anything more to learn. You were never meant to move on from the gospel to something else. Yes, it is where your life as a Christian begins; but it's also where you are meant to stay as a person who follows Jesus. Martin Luther, a German theologian in the 1500s and a key

---

[1] J. D. Greear, *Gospel* (Nashville, TN: B&H Publishing, 2011), 5.

influencer in the beginning of the Protestant Reformation, said about this, "to progress is always to begin again." His point is that for a Christian to continue progressing, or growing, in his or her life with Jesus, he or she must return to the beginning where it all started: the gospel.

So, let's take a few moments to begin again.

You are an image bearer of God. It is important that you remember this truth throughout this book and, more important, throughout your life. You bear God's image. You are valuable and treasured.

In Genesis 1:27 we see that God created people in perfection and in His image. Then, in Genesis 3 we see the first sinful act of humanity. That sinful act had immediate consequences for Adam and Eve, and it has lasting consequences for us today. From that moment forward, all those born of a man and woman inherit a sinful nature. This sinful nature brings with it some of the same consequences that Adam and Eve experienced: death and separation from God. We don't enter life in a neutral place before God; there's no such thing. A person is either in relationship with God or separated from Him. Contrary to popular belief, there's no middle ground.

Romans 3:23 says, "For all have sinned and fall short of the glory of God." Every person enters this life separated from God because of sin. The Bible explains that we are helpless (Rom. 5:6), enemies of God (Rom. 5:10), that we are alienated from Him (Col. 1:21), and deserving of His wrath because of our sin (Eph. 2:3). The post-Genesis 3 picture is pretty bleak.

Since that first act of rebellion against God, sin has brought devastation to people's lives. It has brought devastation to my own life through the separation that exists with God upon entering this world, and it has brought devastation through my own choices to sin. Sin only brings devastation, and its offspring is more sin and more devastation.

At this moment in your life, you are about to be exposed to more opportunity to sin and more kinds of sin than at any point in your life previously. The college campus can be rampant with drunkenness, drugs, and sexual sin, and your choices in these years—whether to participate or to abstain—will have long-lasting consequences for you. You need to understand that what happens in college does not stay in college.

At this point it would be easy to wallow in our sinful state and go on and on about how sinful we are, and some people do. This would be a mistake. It is necessary for us to realize our sin because we can never understand the depth of our salvation until we understand the depth of our sin, but sin isn't the main character of the story. Yes, sin has tainted the good picture that we saw at creation, but God is working to restore His image fully in us. He loves us so much that He provided a way for us to be with Him again rather than leave us in an alienated state before Him. He would rather have us as His children than His enemies.

We are more sinful that we will ever know, but at the same time, we are more loved than we could ever imagine.

He loves us so much, in fact, that He made a way for us to be back in a right relationship with Him. Romans 6:23 sums up this idea perfectly: "For the wages of sin is death, but the gift of God is eternal life in Christ Jesus our Lord." Sin brings death; Jesus brings life. Sin has taken us far away from God; Jesus has made it possible for us to be brought near to Him and into His family.

John 3:16 says it this way: "For God loved the world in this way: He gave his one and only Son, so that everyone who believes in him will not perish but have eternal life." You've probably heard that passage a million times before, and because of that, you may have read through it quickly when you recognized it. Take a moment and look at this verse one more time. Slow down and read every word, absorbing its depth and meaning. Remember, "to progress is always to begin again."

Paul writes in Romans 5:10: "For if, while we were enemies, we were reconciled to God through the death of his Son, then how much more, having been reconciled, will we be saved by his life." Now we begin to see the solution that God brings to the problem of sin: the life, death, and resurrection of His Son, Jesus. Remember that sin causes death. It was one of the original consequences for Adam and Eve in Genesis 3 and it remains for us today. When a person dies without believing in Jesus, the separation from God because of sin in this life is extended for all of eternity. But because of Jesus, we no longer have to experience separation from God in life or death. Jesus makes it possible for a person who is an enemy of God and far from Him to be brought near to Him and adopted into His family. That is what it means to be reconciled to God. The relationship that was broken because of sin is repaired and you can have a relationship with God as His child.

That brings us to an important question that I hope is on your mind: *What exactly did Jesus do to bring about this reconciliation?* This is a question that I hope you spend years rather than minutes answering.

One of the greatest things about our faith is that each time we go to God's Word, He can teach us about who He is and what He has done. So, rather than give an exhaustive answer to this question (which would fill libraries full of books!) I hope what we talk about here leads you to further study.[2] But in order to understand the gospel, it is important that we mention several things Jesus did in order to reconcile us to God.

First, Jesus was born of a virgin. You really only hear about this around Christmas, which is unfortunate, because it is a very important part of Jesus' identity and His ability to reconcile us to

---

[2] For the person and work of Christ, I can think of a few resources: *Jesus the King* by Timothy Keller; *The Cross of Christ* by John Stott; and *The Person of Christ* by Donald MacLeod.

God. The virgin birth means that Jesus is the Son of God, which means He was born without sin. Because Mary's pregnancy was an act of God and not man, Jesus didn't enter His life on earth with the same fallen, corrupt nature that we have.

Second, Jesus lived a perfect life without sin. We see in the Bible that Jesus was tempted to sin by Satan himself (Matt. 4:1–11) and that Jesus was "tempted in every way as we are" (Heb. 4:15). Have you ever thought about the truth that Jesus was tempted in every way, just as we are tempted? Obviously, Jesus didn't have the Internet and He wasn't in a fraternity, so this can't mean all the external circumstances were the same. What this verse is teaching us is that *categorically* Jesus experienced temptation in the same areas that we do. He was tempted sexually, with pride, with anger, with overindulgence, and much more. Sometime the tendency is to think that Jesus just floated through life on a cloud and then ended up on a cross, but that is completely false. He was tempted in every way—He experienced grief, joy, laughter, and the full range of emotions that we experience, because He was fully man. Indeed, He was the perfect man, living this life without sinning in any circumstance.

Third, He died as a substitute for our sin. The consequence, or "wages" of sin, as we see in Romans 6:23, is death. We are guilty of sin and the penalty for that guilt is death. I am guilty of sin and so my penalty is death. That is the judgment against each one of us.

But Jesus, having lived a perfect life, took that perfect life to an execution sentence on a cross. It was there that He died as our substitute. He lived the life that we failed to live and died the death that we deserved to die, so that we could have eternal life with God. To make it personal, He stood in my place as one who was innocent, and said, "I will take his guilty verdict and his penalty in his place."

When we believe in Jesus, a great shift takes place in our lives because of this moment. God, the righteous Judge, moves our

guilty verdict and our sin to Jesus so that the penalty can be right-
fully paid. In that same moment, Jesus' perfect life and innocence
is given to us so that we can be brought into God's family.

I hope you're seeing how these things fit together. If Jesus
had not been born of a virgin—if He had been only a human
and not also God—there would have been a corrupted nature,
which would have disqualified Him from being our substitute. If
Jesus had sinned in His life, it would have disqualified Him from
being our substitute. If He had not died, then the penalty for sin
would not have been paid by a perfect sacrifice. And all of this
was done so that God could fully reveal His love, grace, mercy,
and forgiveness, and reconcile us to Himself, transforming us from
His enemies to His children.

Fourth, Jesus rose from the dead, conquering death and
securing our salvation. Most often when people talk about the
resurrection of Christ, the focus is on it securing our future resurrection. This is true, but I want to focus your attention on how
the resurrection is the final punctuation to Jesus' work of reconciliation. There are two specific passages that I want to point you
to for this: 1 Corinthians 15:17 and Romans 4:25. These passages
teach us that without Jesus' resurrection, we would still be in our
sin and that Jesus was raised from the dead for our justification.
We will talk more about justification in the next chapter, but the
basic meaning is that we are declared not guilty for our sin, and
are rather declared to be righteous before God. Remember the
life-switch that I mentioned just a moment ago? There is a guilt
switch that takes place at the same time where Jesus takes upon
Himself the guilt of our sin and we are given His innocence and
righteousness. In its simplest form, that is justification, and without the resurrection, we can't be justified. This miracle—God the
Father raising His Son from the dead—is the final statement on
His work of bringing salvation, forgiveness, and eternal life to us,
His people.

As J. D. Greear was quoted earlier: This is the gospel, "the announcement that God has reconciled us to Himself by sending His Son Jesus to die as a substitute for our sins, and that all who repent and believe have eternal life in Him."

This may be the first time you've heard about sin, Jesus, and His work to reconcile us to God. Or you may have heard this before, but for the first time in your life you've actually *heard* the gospel in a way that makes sense to you. My prayer for you as you've read and perhaps re-read this chapter is that God opens your heart to believe in Him, which you can do right now. Here. As you sit with this book, you can believe in Jesus and be transformed from an enemy of God, who is far from Him, to a child of God, a member of His family. The great switch of guilt and perfection can happen to you. Here is what it takes, according to Romans 10:9–10: "If you confess with your mouth, 'Jesus is Lord,' and believe in your heart that God raised Him from the dead, you will be saved." Will you pray a prayer to God right now, expressing these things?

Just as I understand that there are people reading this book who may not believe in Jesus, I know that you may be someone who has already believed. My prayer for you in this chapter is that the gospel has become fresh to you again and that it becomes something that isn't forgotten or traded in for some other "deep truth." The reality is, there is no deeper truth than this. The gospel is not just for one moment of our spiritual life; it is meant to be our strength to obey and the filter by which we live. It doesn't just get us started in the Christian life; it gets us all the way home. As you understand more about the gospel, it will move you to worship, obey, and follow Jesus to a greater degree, and by experiencing these things, you will be able to live these very important years of your life differently from those around you.

Believer, the gospel is not through with you yet. There is much more to experience about the impact it can have on your daily life, which is exactly where we are headed in the next chapter.

# Chapter 2

# Life with the Gospel

**THE GOSPEL ISN'T THROUGH** with you, and you shouldn't be through with it. Yet, many Christians stop thinking about the gospel after the moment of their salvation and move on to learn or accomplish other Christian things. Moving on from the gospel is not something we're meant to do. It's the announcement of what reconciles us to God *and* it provides us the strength that we need to live each day. Knowing the gospel, understanding the gospel, diving deeper into the gospel, and meditating on the gospel is the key to experiencing the abundant life that Jesus said He came to give us in John 10:10.

Have you ever stopped to think about what it takes to live an abundant or full life? The college experience, as our society defines it, is a shortcut to the "abundant life"—the so-called abundant life of experiencing everything you can during these years. As much sex as you can with as many people as you can. As much partying as you can. Dabbling in anything that comes your way. The thought is that these are the years that you have to experiment with anything and everything—and that this is "abundant" living.

That college experience may be fun for a season, but it only leads to pain, scars, baggage, and consequences that last long after your college years.

There is a different way, and it is incredibly rewarding, exciting, and joy-filled. That kind of college experience, what I would submit to you is the only worthwhile college experience, is lived with your eyes firmly focused on Jesus.

## The Importance of Obedience

We are an easily distracted people. Maybe you remember the movie *Up* from when you were a kid, and the dog who was continually distracted by squirrels. If you've never seen that movie, think back to the most recent time you tried to study for a big exam or write a research paper. Remember how every little thing would pull your attention away from what you were trying to accomplish? The same is true in our relationship with God: we are easily distracted.

The next several years of your life in college will bring more distraction than you've experienced before. It's in those moments of distraction that we can find ourselves in compromising situations and most susceptible to sin. Remember that sin only brings destruction and leads to more sin, which takes us away from an abundant life. So, if sin takes us away from the abundant life Jesus means for us to have, then the opposite action must lead us toward the abundant life: following Jesus and living in obedience to Him.

Throughout the Bible we see God commanding His people to obey Him. It is a pervasive theme throughout the Old Testament as we follow the story line of God's people and how God was orchestrating His plan to reconcile His people to Himself through Jesus. Then, as Jesus enters the world, we continue to see the command for the people of God to obey Him. In John 14:15 Jesus says plainly, "If you love me, you will keep my commands." We see similar commands in John 14:23, 1 John 5:2, 1 Peter 2:9, Luke 11:28, 2 John 1:6, and a host of others. The Bible is clear: if someone loves Him, follows Him, has been reconciled to Him, has been saved by Him (and so on), then that person will obey God.

You may be thinking at this point, *Obeying Jesus all the time doesn't sound like abundant life. In fact, it sounds very restricting, and abundant life is all about freedom.* You're right—there are restrictions placed on us by Jesus. But here's the thing: we all have restrictions placed on us by whatever we love most.

If what you love most is excelling in your education so you can get a great job, you'll have to spend extra time in the library and be restricted from hanging out with your friends. If what you love most is achieving status and popularity, you'll have to spend extra time hanging out with friends and be restricted from that extra time studying. If you're an athlete and what you love most is being the best player on your team, your diet, exercise, and sleep will have to be rigorous, and will restrict you in other ways.

Following Jesus is no different, except for one thing: the restrictions that Jesus gives us actually bring more freedom. How is this possible? All the other things we love are created, so the restrictions they place on us are from one created thing to another. School and status and sports don't know what's best for us. But the restrictions God places on us are from our Creator, and He does know what is best for us. As Timothy Keller puts it, God's "directives are from your *designer*. And therefore they aren't busywork. To break them is to violate your own nature and to lose freedom, just like a person who eats the wrong foods and ends up in a hospital."[1]

You need to know that your obedience to God through His Word is important, and as a follower of Jesus, you should be continually growing in obedience to Him. This isn't always easy and it doesn't happen right away. We must learn to obey God, just like we would learn to do anything else in our lives, and the great news for you is that God has provided the way for you to grow in your obedience to Him.

---

[1] Timothy Keller, *Making Sense of God* (New York: Penguin Books, 2016), 115.

## Sanctification: Growing in Obedience

The process of learning to obey God and growing in our obedience is something the Bible refers to as "sanctification." There are two sides to this word. The first side is something that happens the moment a person first believes in Jesus. Because of Jesus' perfect life, sacrifice, and resurrection, God declares us not guilty of our sin (justification from chapter 1) and at the same time He also declares us perfect and holy. God sees you as holy because He sees you through His Son. Right now, in terms of standing before God, you as a believer in Jesus are as holy as you will ever be. It's so important to let that truth sink in because it changes everything about the way you approach growing in obedience to God. You don't obey God to acquire more holiness. You don't obey God to make Him happy or to keep Him from being angry with you. He already sees you as holy because of Jesus. Obedience to God has nothing to do with us earning anything; it's all been earned for us by Jesus. This means that the Christian life is not about waking up every day and trying harder or willing yourself to obey God, but instead learning to live out who God has already said you are through Jesus.

While the first side of sanctification isn't something you participate in, you do participate in the second side. The sanctification that you experience in this life is the actual process of growing in your obedience to God. It is the process you are on to become more like Jesus, to become more holy throughout your lifetime. Here's what that process looks like visually:[2]

---

[2] Wayne Grudem, *Bible Doctrine* (Grand Rapids, MI: 1999), 329.

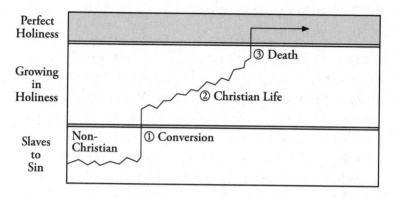

**The Process of Sanctification**

Nathan Bingham from Ligonier Ministries says it this way: "Sanctification is growth. In regeneration [when you first believe in Jesus], God implants desires that were not there before: desire for God, for holiness, and for glorifying God's name in the world; desire to pray and worship; desire to love and bring benefit to others."[3] These are desires that we don't create or conjure up; they are given to us, "implanted" within us as a gift from God at salvation. As these desires grow, so will your obedience to God, and God has provided the way for these desires to continue growing in you.

### The Holy Spirit: The One Who Helps You Obey

In John 14:15–17, Jesus reveals how this works. He says,

> "If you love me, you will keep my commands. And I will ask the Father, and he will give you another Counselor to be with you forever. He is the Spirit of truth. The world is unable to receive him because it doesn't see him or know him. But

---

[3] Nathan Bingham, "What Is Sanctification," Ligonier Ministries, June 24, 2013; https://www.ligonier.org/blog/what-sanctification/.

you do know him, because he remains with you
and will be in you."

Once again, we see the link between loving God and obeying
His commands, which He restates again in John 14:23–24.

In the midst of this link between loving God and obeying
Him, Jesus introduces the Holy Spirit, whom He refers to as the
"Counselor" and the "Spirit of truth." The Holy Spirit can sometimes seem mysterious to people. Some think of Him as a ghost
or something similar, and few truly understand His role in the
life of a follower of Jesus. Unfortunately, churches rarely teach on
the Holy Spirit, and those that do often misunderstand Him and
teach on Him to the exclusion of the Father and Son. As a result,
you may be in a place where you understand very little about Him.
Here are some basics.

The Holy Spirit is part of the Trinity: God the Father, God
the Son, and God the Holy Spirit. All are equal and each one
of them is fully God, yet at the same time, all are the same God.
There are three persons in the Trinity, but only one God.

Here is another point where I would plead with you to take
up study on your own.[4] There is a depth here that is beautiful to
explore and it will do you well, but because of the context of this
particular book, I want to focus our attention to some specific
ways the Holy Spirit helps grow our desires to love and obey God.

First, the Holy Spirit is always present with you. Jesus says
that the Holy Spirit will be with you forever and will remain in
you. This happens for you at the moment of your belief in Jesus.
The Holy Spirit takes up residence in you and will remain with
you forever, meaning that what He is meant to do in your life He
will continue to do for you forever. This is the foundation for the

---

[4] For further resources, see *Rediscovering the Holy Spirit* by Michael
Horton; *The Holy Spirit* by Sinclair Ferguson; *The Mystery of the Holy Spirit*
by R. C. Sproul; and *Forgotten God* by Francis Chan.

different roles of the Holy Spirit, and it is incredibly important. God will never leave you because He has placed His Spirit within you. You never have to be alone again.

Loneliness is an epidemic on college campuses. In a recent study, the American College Health Association found that, of twenty-eight thousand college students surveyed, 60 percent had felt "very lonely" within the last twelve months. Thirty percent of this group also reported that they felt "very lonely" within the last two weeks of when the survey was given.[5] In a similar survey conducted by the National College Health Assessment, 44 percent of forty-eight thousand college students said they felt "so depressed that it was difficult to function."[6]

I could continue to throw statistics at you that would prove this point, but chances are, you don't need them, because you've felt the loneliness yourself. Maybe you are reading this book within the first couple of weeks on a new campus and you are being hit particularly hard by loneliness in this moment. Loneliness can be very dangerous for you emotionally, spiritually, and even physically. Dietrich Bonhoeffer said, "Sin demands to have a man by himself."[7] When we are lonely, we are more likely to sin. When we are lonely, we are more likely to lower our standards in order to remove the loneliness. When we are lonely, we are more likely to continue to spiral downward emotionally. All this is because we as people weren't meant to be alone, which we will talk about at greater length later in the book.

The good news is, God has provided a way through the Holy Spirit that you will never be alone. He, the God of the universe, is with you, and wants to have a relationship with you. Not a mysterious "talking to the air" type of relationship, but an actual

---

[5] www.acha.org/ACHA

[6] www.acha.org/ncha

[7] Dietrich Bonhoeffer, *Life Together: The Classic Exploration of Christian Community* (New York: HarperOne, 1954).

relationship where you know He is close, where you hear from Him, and are confident that He hears you.

There's a lot of meaning behind the title Jesus gives to the Holy Spirit in John 14. Jesus refers to Him as the "Counselor." This word can also mean comforter and advocate. God places the Holy Spirit within your life to counsel you, comfort you, and advocate for you, and He will do these things forever.

Interestingly, the word that the Bible often uses for Satan means "accuser." It's as if you're in a court of law, and Satan's main attack on you is accusation. He's always accusing you of your sin, accusing you of not being good enough, accusing you of not measuring up.

But who else is in the courtroom? The Holy Spirit. Your advocate. And when Satan tempts you to doubt, to despair, or to forget the gospel, the Holy Spirit is right there, advocating on your behalf, reminding you, "There is now no condemnation for those in Christ Jesus" (Rom. 8:1). You are a sinner, but your sin has been completely forgiven because of Christ. You aren't good enough, but Jesus was good enough on your behalf. You can't measure up, but Jesus measured up perfectly, and when the Father looks at you, that's what He sees.

The second way the Holy Spirit helps you grow in your obedience to God is by teaching you. As you saw in the passage earlier, Jesus refers to the Holy Spirit as the Spirit of truth. Later in this same conversation, Jesus says the Holy Spirit will "teach you all things and remind you of everything I have told you" (John 14:26). The Holy Spirit guides you to the truth so that you can understand and obey it.

Have you ever felt like reading the Bible was difficult or confusing? I have as well, and more than likely will again. Everyone begins in that place and then experiences it at times throughout their life as a follower of Jesus. Part of that is because there is such a depth to God's Word that you can literally spend a lifetime of discovery within its pages. For the majority of people, however, the Bible is difficult or confusing because they have simply not put the time into it to learn.

Studying the Bible is a discipline that takes practice and many put it down at the first sign of difficulty. But studying chemistry takes work, studying calculus takes work, studying Shakespeare takes work—why would we expect the Bible to be easy? Here's what I want you to know: with some work, you can understand it, because the Holy Spirit is in you. The more time you spend in God's Word, the more comfortable you will become with it, which will help you develop the ability to listen to what the Holy Spirit is teaching you through it.

I've talked with hundreds of students throughout my time in student ministry about reading the Bible, and there is one common issue that rises to the top among the ones who struggle to consistently spend time in God's Word: they read the Bible like any other book, rather than reading it like a conversation expecting to hear back from it. The Bible is not like any other book. The author (God) wants to speak to you through it, and the Holy Spirit within you helps make that possible.[8]

One of my favorite verses in the Bible is 2 Corinthians 3:18, which says, "We all, with unveiled faces, are looking as in a mirror at the glory of the Lord and are being transformed into the same image from glory to glory; this is from the Lord who is the Spirit." As you grow in your obedience to Him, your life is transformed to resemble the life of Jesus more and more. Remember that Jesus earned the perfect life for you and the sanctification that you are living in now is a constant growth, a transformation into what Jesus has earned for you. This verse gives us the formula for that transformation: in order for your life to be transformed, you must stare at Jesus.

---

[8] For further study, I recommend Jen Wilkin's *Women of the Word* and Rob Plummer's *40 Questions about Interpreting the Bible*.

Did you catch that from the verse? The picture is this: you are staring at a mirror, and in that mirror is the glory of Jesus. As you look at it, you are transformed into the image that you see. Your transformation, or growth in obedience to God, is directly linked to how much you are staring at Jesus.

Right now, you should be asking yourself, "How do I stare at Jesus?" The answer is *through the Bible*. When you spend time in God's Word, you are "staring at Jesus," looking into that mirror and learning about Him, His commands, and the plan that God had from the beginning pages to redeem His people through Jesus. As you stare at Jesus through the Bible, the Holy Spirit reveals truth to you so that you can grow in your obedience and become more and more transformed into the image of Jesus. Yet, there are few who stare at Jesus adequately.

There are different ways you can look at someone. The first is the elevator glance. You know it. It's the one that you use when you get onto an elevator when someone else is already there. It is a brief glance and a slight nod of the head followed by scooting over to the side of the elevator as far away from them as possible. There may or may not be words used, but in every case it is a very brief interaction with very little eye contact. Why? Because prolonged eye contact in an elevator is just weird and you should get off at the next floor.

The second look is one that you give an acquaintance in the hallway or out in public somewhere when you don't want to stop and talk but you still want to acknowledge their presence in the world. This look involves brief eye contact, perhaps a more enthused head nod, but not too much, so you can still avoid stopping.

The third look is called the three-second stare and is used only when you want to make sure the person you are looking at knows you're interested. It's the kind of look that makes you want to walk across the room and introduce yourself to someone. It's a look that feels more intense because you lock eyes with someone for three seconds or longer, which can feel like an eternity. It's a look that says, "I really like what I see," in a completely non-creepy way.

Too many times in our lives we are satisfied with giving Jesus an elevator glance or a head nod instead of staring at Him with the intensity and focus that He deserves, and as a result, the growth in our obedience to God is stunted and warped. You cannot obey God and grow in your sanctification without staring at Jesus, and the main way to stare at Him is through His Word.

An amazing thing happens when you take the time to stare at Jesus: you begin to love Him more, and that is the key issue here. I said earlier that the Christian life isn't about getting up every day, trying harder, and willing yourself to obey God. It isn't. It isn't even about obeying God first and foremost. It is first about looking to Jesus as the "source and perfecter of our faith" (Heb. 12:2). He is the source, the beginning and starting point of our faith through the gospel, as we saw in the previous chapter. He is also the perfecter of our faith, the finisher of it. He is the one who brings it to completion within us (Phil. 1:6). That completion involves us growing in obedience and being transformed to be more like Jesus as we stare at Him through His Word, but make sure you notice it begins with Jesus, not your actions.

Back in John 14:15 and 23, we saw that a love for Jesus precludes obedience to Him: "if you love, then you will obey." All of these passages affirm one truth for us: the pursuit of the Christian life begins as a pursuit to love Jesus more, not as a pursuit to obey Him. Growing in obedience is the result of a growing love for Jesus that only comes as we know Him more and more.

The reality for each of us is that every day, we stare at *something*, and that something has a transformational impact on us. It may be a boyfriend or girlfriend; it may be status and popularity; it may be success in the classroom. We will stare at whatever we love most, and whatever that is, it will change us. It may be yourself, your feelings of guilt, your broken family. Life is full of distractions that will try to pull your eyes away from Jesus, and as a believer who has the Holy Spirit within them, you must learn to pull your eyes back to Jesus through His Word.

So far we have seen that the Holy Spirit helps us to grow in our obedience to God by being with us forever as our counselor, comforter, and advocate. We've also seen that He teaches us truth as we read God's Word. Closely connected to this second way the Spirit helps us is the third. Jesus tells us—back again in John 14:26—that the Holy Spirit reminds us of everything that He has told us.

When you spend time in God's Word long enough to learn to listen to the Holy Spirit and long enough to stare intently at what He has to teach you, you will notice that His Word comes to your mind as you go throughout the day. The Holy Spirit will bring Scriptures to your mind to help you fight against sin and will convict you of moments of sin in order to help you fix your eyes back on Jesus. As your comforter, the Holy Spirit will remind you of Jesus' love for you, His actions toward you, and how He has saved you.

Let's take a look at Romans 8:12–17 to see these things at work. Paul, the author of Romans, begins by making clear that there is a difference between living according to the flesh and living according to the Spirit. These are common terms in Scripture that describe pre-salvation living (in sin) and post-salvation living, where the Spirit is dwelling in the believer. In verse 13 Paul says, "But if by the Spirit you put to death the deeds of the body, you will live." As you learn to listen to the Spirit through God's Word, you will develop a deep well of Scripture that the Holy Spirit can draw on to remind you of truth, helping you "put to death" the sin in your life. In exchange, the Spirit will give you godly thoughts, helping you "set your minds on things above"

(Col. 3:2). This exchange, the Bible says, results in *life*. We can understand that to mean the abundant life that we talked about at the start of this chapter.

Your college experience can be an amazing, joy-filled, abundant life here on earth as the Spirit helps you put sin to death and grow in obedience.

In Romans 8:16, we see another special action of the Holy Spirit, as "The Spirit himself testifies together with our spirit that we are God's children." The Holy Spirit is with you forever to remind you that you are part of God's family. That can never be taken away from you and you can never be separated from His love for you (Rom. 8:31–39). You have been brought from far away as an enemy into a close relationship with Him as His child. We see that in the gospel for salvation and we see it each day from that point forward, as the Holy Spirit reminds us, comforts us, counsels us, and fixes our eyes on Jesus, so that we can learn to love Him more.

# Part 2

# Identity

# Chapter 3

# Your View of God and God's View of You

**YOUR VIEW OF GOD** is the most important thing about you.

I heard this phrase for the first time as a twenty-three-year-old student pastor, and it has come to be one of the most impactful statements that I've ever heard. It is adapted from the popular A. W. Tozer quote: "What comes into our minds when we think about God is the most important thing about us." It's something my pastor at the time, Buddy Gray, used to say frequently, and I wish I'd heard it years earlier. That phrase, and that pastor, challenged me to dive deeper into a discovery of who God is, and it changed my life. It still impacts me to this day. I've come to know the truth of that statement as I've lived with it, and my hope is that you will come to know the truth of it as well, because this single statement can be the difference-maker in your college experience.

Here's a question I want you to think about. Take the time to pause in your reading of this book and think about your answer. Write your thoughts down in a journal or even make some notes in the margin of this page. Here's the question: *What comes into your mind when you think about God?*

You may be new to this whole idea of God and a relationship with Him, or you may be someone that has heard about God your entire life. The reality for each person, regardless of where you currently fall on the knowledge-of-God spectrum, is that you will only devote your life to something that you believe is worthy of your worship.

Each of us chooses to worship something, to place something as the ultimate in our lives. For some in your stage of life, the college experience becomes the ultimate. Experiencing anything and everything takes the place of God. For others it is a career, a relationship, an addiction, or even religion. Whatever becomes the ultimate in your life will cause you to make decisions that move you more toward that ultimate.

When you discover that God is the only One deserving of your worship, your decisions will begin to be shaped around worshipping Him as the ultimate in your life. That's why we chose to begin this book with two chapters that focus specifically on the gospel instead of focusing on a list of things that we think you need to do and a list of things you need to avoid in order to have a quality college experience. A right understanding of the gospel will lead you to a bigger view of God, which will increase your desire to worship Him as the ultimate, which will lead to a lifestyle that begins to look more like Jesus.

Many religious people start with a list, because we are naturally people. Perhaps you grew up in a Christian context like this—less about loving Jesus, more about mustering up the ability to obey Him. When we hear things like "live the Christian life" or "sanctification journey," we immediately want to know what we have to do in order to accomplish it. Certainly, the Bible tells us things that we need to do and things that we need to avoid in order to obey Him, but if life with Jesus is nothing more than a morality checklist, then that morality becomes our ultimate instead of God, and when morality becomes ultimate, we set ourselves up for a spiritually depressed existence, because there will always be moments when we can't live according to the list.

Perhaps you grew up in church and you feel like your Christian life has been lived on a treadmill, constantly running and never getting anywhere. More than likely, this is because you were taught that your life as a follower of Jesus is all about the morality list. This is the way I grew up and lived until that pastor challenged me to think otherwise. What I learned is that a morality checklist isn't the source of my Christian life, God is—and as my view of Him grows, my life will grow closer to Him, and my decisions will begin to fall in line with what He says in His Word. That's why the most important thing about me is my view of God. A morality list leads you into slavery and depression. A growing view of God leads you into freedom and a full life.

## Another Piece of the Puzzle?

In the last chapter, we talked about the vital role that God's Word plays in your sanctification journey. It's the way that you fix your eyes on Jesus, and it is the primary way that your view of God grows. The Bible is the place where you begin to discover who God is so that you begin to stand in awe of Him. This place of awe, amazement, or worship will become the foundation that your relationships, career, daily decisions, and college experience will be built upon.

It's been helpful in the past for me to think about this process like putting together a puzzle. Chances are, when you were a kid, you learned to put together a puzzle the way just about everyone else learns: you start with the frame. This is because the frame is the most important part. It gives you a clear starting point, serves as a guide for the rest of the puzzle, and supports the rest of the puzzle pieces in their final state.

You have a lot of puzzle pieces in your life right now, and you're trying to figure out where they belong. There are pieces that you had in high school that you've carried to this point and you are discovering more and more pieces every day as you move through your college experience. Whatever is ultimate in your life will serve as the frame that everything else clings to, and for too many Christians, God is just another puzzle piece, rather than the frame itself. When God is just another puzzle piece to you, things will never seem to fit correctly, because God doesn't fit as just another piece next to some class you are taking, a current relationship, or your part-time job. God is meant to be the frame. That's the only place that He fits, and it is the only way that the other pieces in your life will begin to make sense and fit together. The only way that God becomes the frame for your life is when you are driven to stand in awe and worship of Him.

I want us to pause for another moment to give you some time to stop and stand in awe of God. I want you to read these Scriptures and take the time to reflect on them in light of what we've been talking about. Focus on God and your view of who He is, then make some notes about what you learn about Him from these Scriptures. Write those notes in a journal or notepad.

*Isaiah 6:1–8*          *John 3:16–17*
*Ephesians 2:1–10*     *Genesis 1–2:3*
*Job 38–39*

## Love God with All Your Mind

Alongside of Scripture itself, one thing that has helped me to develop a bigger view of God is the study of theology and doctrine. I know what you are probably thinking, and I am aware that you have homework, that you are busy, and that you aren't looking for yet another assignment, but this one is worth it. There are a multitude of theology-related books that you can dive into and expand your knowledge of God. A common misunderstanding is that the Christian life is all faith and feeling without any intellectual contribution. Salvation is by faith alone in Jesus, but that faith introduces you to God for the first time, and as you begin to know God, there will be a desire within you to begin the pursuit of knowing God more. Much of that pursuit will cause you to flex your intellectual muscles as you study the Bible, as well as theology and doctrine.[1]

Too many Christians go through life with too small a view of God because they refuse to engage their mind in their Christian life. This isn't just a small issue—it's a direct command from Jesus in Luke 10:27: "Love the Lord your God with all your heart, with all your soul, with all your strength, and with all your *mind*," and "your neighbor as yourself" (emphasis mine). This command isn't given to us so that we become a group of intellectual elitist Christians who look down on everyone else. It is given to us because "The more we know about God, His Word, and His relationships to the world and mankind, the better we will trust Him, the more fully we will praise Him, and the more readily we will obey Him."[2]

## A New Identity

As you begin to study Scripture and doctrine, loving God with all your mind, you will begin to see more of how God views you. Everyone is seeking an identity or something to be known for. This process begins as early as the toddler ages and is clearly seen when small children want to be the fastest, biggest, and generally to be the best at everything. They are searching for identity.

You are too, but in a different way. You may have already come to grips with the reality that you aren't the fastest person or the best at coloring pictures—but you are searching for an identity, because that is the way college is structured. You are out on your own for

---

[1] Here are some books I would recommend, some on the light side, some heavier: *Systematic Theology* by John Frame, *Systematic Theology* by Wayne Grudem, *Christian Beliefs* by Wayne Grudem, *The Story of Christianity* by Justo Gonzalez, *The Reason for God* by Timothy Keller, and *Desiring God* by John Piper.

[2] Wayne Grudem, *Bible Doctrine* (Grand Rapids, MI: Zondervan, 1999), 23.

the first time, preparing for what you will one day become. Nobody cares anymore what you were known for in high school. The college experience is all about creating a new identity for yourself.

If you are feeling some uncertainty about what to do with your life and what this new identity will be, you're not alone. It is a common place to be in the beginning years of college, and sometimes even extends far beyond the college years. There are some positive things to this journey because it forces you to ask some hard questions of yourself, like what exactly your life is going to be about from this point forward. This moment in your life gives you the opportunity to do things differently if you have regrets remaining from your high school years. This uncertainty can also bring about some real challenges, as this uncertainty leads many people into an experimental mind-set. They begin trying to "find themselves" in anything and everything. This experimental approach to finding and crafting identity is an unquenchable thirst that only leads to a deeper spiral of searching without finding answers. Read the book of Ecclesiastes—even Solomon figured this out three thousand years ago.

You don't have to live that kind of college experience. For the person who believes in Jesus, there are answers to this identity uncertainty found in the gospel and how God views you. He has made you a "new creation" (2 Cor. 5:17) and has given you a new identity.

You are a child of God. John 1:12 says, "But to all who did receive him, he gave them the right to be children of God, to those who believe in his name." As we saw in Romans 8:14–17, we received adoption into God's family and the Holy Spirit constantly reminds us that we are God's children. Galatians 4:4–7 shares a similar truth: "When the time came to completion, God sent his Son, born of a woman, born under the law, to redeem those under the law, so that we might receive adoption as sons. And because you are sons, God sent the Spirit of his Son into our hearts crying 'Abba, Father!' So you are no longer a slave but a son, and if a son then God has made you an heir."

Along with being a child of God, there is another distinction that is made in both the Romans and Galatians passages. As part of this adoption, you are also called an "heir" and "coheir" with Jesus (Rom. 8:17). This is an amazing truth. It means we will have access to everything that Jesus Himself has access and privilege to. God sees you with the same status that He sees Jesus.

We occasionally hear about being an heir or receiving an inheritance in our culture today, but in the time of the Bible it was a frequent theme and occurrence. Typically, the eldest son received the largest portion of the father's possessions when the father died. Other sons would receive decreasing amounts of the inheritance according to their birth order and the total number of sons. What we are being told here in Scripture is that we are coheirs with Christ, meaning that we get the same portion. There isn't a separation of access between what God gives Jesus and what God gives you. You have the full Holy Spirit. You have full access to God in relationship. You have full holiness and perfection in His sight. And when Jesus returns, you will receive a new heaven and new earth; a glorified, perfect, remade physical body; and eternity with the Father.

You are a child of God forever. Take a look at Ephesians 1:13–14: "In him you also were sealed with the promised Holy Spirit when you heard the word of truth, the gospel of your salvation, and when you believed. The Holy Spirit is the down payment of our inheritance, until the redemption of the possession, to the praise of his glory." We've talked a good bit about the Holy Spirit so far, and this seal or guarantee of your salvation is another role that He plays.

Throughout your life, the Spirit is there to protect your new identity, to preserve what God has done for you, and to remind you that God is always present with you (1 John 4:13). There are moments along the sanctification journey when you may experience doubt. You may doubt God's love for you, that He is with you, or even your own salvation. You aren't the only one who has had those thoughts. There's no shame in walking through seasons of doubt. The temptation in those moments will be to pull away from God because of the guilt or shame you experience, and to pull away from His people. Remember that, through Jesus, your guilt and shame have been healed. Remember also the quote mentioned in the last chapter: "Sin demands to have a man by himself." Times of doubt are not times when you need to retreat, hide, or run away from God or His people in fear. They are times when you need to move closer. They are times when you need to fix your eyes upon Jesus through His Word. They are times when you need to listen to the voice of the Holy Spirit crying out within you, "*Abba*, Father," to remind you that you are a child of God. They are times when you need to draw near to the church, to remind you that you are not an only child, but have brothers and sisters who are there to love and support you. God also wants to listen to you. He is big enough to hear your questions and your doubts. He wants to hear from you because you are His child—forever.

## Grace

You are a child of God through grace. Grace is an attribute of God and is "the way that He deals with His people, not on the basis of their merit or worthiness, what they deserve, but simply according to their need."[3] Another way to say it is that grace is "the free and unmerited favour of God, as manifested in the salvation of sinners and the bestowal of blessings" (*Oxford Dictionary*). It is by God's grace that you became a child of God through faith in Jesus.

---

[3] Millard J. Erickson, *Christian Theology*, 2nd ed. (Grand Rapids, MI: Baker Books, 1998), 320–21.

Ephesians 2:1–10 explains that God displays His "immeasurable" grace through Jesus. God's action toward us in the gospel was an act of grace. Because of sin, we deserved death and separation from God, which is why Ephesians is clear to say that this work of salvation is from God, not from our effort. There isn't anything that we could do to earn God's favor, so Jesus did it for us and as an act of God's grace.

One misunderstanding would be to think that grace stops at salvation. God's immeasurable grace isn't just available to you in that salvation moment, but throughout all of eternity. Grace can be a difficult thing to understand, so I want to take some time to zoom in.

First, grace can be misunderstood because it is contrary to the way our society works. You began learning at a young age about the opposite of grace. You learned that good behavior gets you good rewards, good grades get you more rewards, being good at sports gets you more rewards. In fact, you may be in college right now so you can excel in the classroom, get a good job, and make lots of money (rewards). This may sound like an oversimplification, but it's how our culture works. It's not how grace works. God gives blessings to you based on His own goodness, kindness, and love—not because of anything we do. This is incredibly freeing because it shows us that God isn't waiting to give us blessings, nor is He withholding them from us based on how we performed today. God is going to act in grace toward you because you are His child.

Second, grace can be misunderstood as a license to sin. Because God's grace is based in Himself and not our merit, some believe that they can sin as much as they want, because the pool of immeasurable grace is waiting for them to jump back in and be forgiven again. When you add to this the truth that the Holy Spirit seals us forever as a child of God, it can lead to this very dangerous misunderstanding.

This may sound strange to you, but it is a misunderstanding that has been happening since people first began to understand grace. Paul addresses this very issue in the fifth and sixth chapters of Romans. Check it out:

> The law came along to multiply the trespass. But where sin multiplied, grace multiplied even more so that, just as sin reigned in death, so also grace will reign through righteousness, resulting in eternal life through Jesus Christ our Lord. What should we say then? Should we continue in sin so that grace may multiply? Absolutely not! How can we who died to sin still live in it? (5:20–6:2)

As you can see, Paul quickly addresses the concept of a license to sin, the thought that we should continue living a life of sin so that we can experience more and more grace. His response to this misunderstanding is an emphatic, "Absolutely not!" The reason why this point of view is wrong is given through the question asked here and then explained more in the following verses. The basic point is that the idea of sinning more within the freedom of grace is preposterous because, as Christians, we have died to sin and been made alive in Christ. Sin doesn't rule us anymore. Grace hasn't given you freedom *to* sin; it's given you freedom *from* sin through Jesus! So why would we ever return to a life of sinning? This doesn't mean that as Christians we won't sin at all, but it does mean that we won't live a lifestyle characterized by sin.

You have been made into a new creation through the gospel, by the grace of God, and the more time you spend on the journey of sanctification, the more your heart will begin to detest sin. Grace reveals the way God views you, and it grows your view of God. Grace brings you freedom, grace is there to pick you up when you fall, grace helps you fight against sin, and grace motivates you to love God.

# Chapter 4

# How You View You

**A FIRM UNDERSTANDING OF** how God views you will lead to a healthy view of yourself. As with other things we've discussed, it takes time to develop a healthy view of yourself that is based in God's Word and what He has declared you to be. Our culture has so warped the idea of identity that there are few who develop a healthy view of themselves that leads to growth in following Jesus. Instead, a warped identity can lead you into destructive behavior that manifests itself in specific ways in the college years.

There's so much emphasis placed on your college experience being the place where you find yourself or begin to develop yourself. You are expected to get an education that provides you with a successful career, and, in many cases, you are expected to find someone that you will one day marry and have a family with. Those are massive burdens of expectation that can be crippling, and it isn't the college experience that you are meant to have. Yes, education is important, and if you meet someone that you will one day marry, that's a great thing too. But your identity is not based in your ability to deliver on those expectations, or any other expectations for that matter. The American dream has taught you for your entire life that you have to be the best, win at everything, and make the most money—and it's a lie. Succumbing to those burdens of expectation will lead you away from Jesus and damage how you view your relationship with Him.

## Two Extremes

In general, there are two extremes in how people view themselves, and every person naturally drifts toward one or the other. You can probably guess what they are, and as we talk through them together I want you to think about which extreme you naturally drift toward.

The first extreme is when a person thinks too highly of him or herself. We've all known people like this. They are the ones who believe that their skills and abilities will take them wherever they want to go in life. They believe they will be successful at anything they touch and they don't need anyone else's help along the way. This person is supremely confident to the point of arrogance.

The Bible has many things to say about the person who lives in this extreme. Proverbs 16:5 says, "Everyone with a proud heart is detestable to the LORD; be assured, he will not go unpunished." James 4:6 says, "God resists the proud, but gives grace to the humble." You might read those and think, *Wow, that is strong language and action coming from God.* Indeed, it is.

The point here is that the proud person believes they don't need God. They haven't yet come to the place where they see their sin, because nothing they do is wrong; because they haven't recognized their sin, they haven't recognized their need for a Savior. This person is still an enemy of God and far from Him.

The second extreme is when a person thinks too lowly of him or herself. This person believes that he or she doesn't have any real value. He is continually self-deprecating; she is constantly speaking or thinking badly about herself. People like this may also be high achievers, but it is only because they are trying to achieve or find success in order to bring themselves out of the pit they've put themselves in. On the other hand, they may have decided to just give up and float through life aimlessly and hopelessly.

When Jesus speaks of giving grace to the humble, this is not what He means. Humility from a biblical perspective is not thinking of yourself higher than you should, like the first extreme I mentioned, but humility is also not thinking less of yourself than you should. Humility is simply thinking of yourself less. C. S. Lewis was right when he said that a truly humble person "will not be thinking about humility; he will not be thinking about himself at all."[1] This true humility is very different than the extreme of considering yourself lowly, worthless, or a constant failure.

Remember when I asked you to think about which one of these extremes you naturally drift toward? It is an important question because the point of view you are coming from will determine how you approach God and the salvation He offers through Jesus. Each extreme brings unique challenges. The proud person tends to believe she doesn't need God; the self-deprecating person tends to believe that there's no way God would ever want to have a relationship with him.

There are a lot of factors that can contribute to the way people view themselves, and if you're stuck viewing yourself in one of these two ways—especially at an extreme or obsessive level—my advice for you is to find a professional, biblical counselor to begin seeing. This isn't a counseling book, and I'm not a professional counselor, but I believe in the process. It's healthy for people to walk through these things alongside others who are trained to help, and who guide you from a Christ-centered perspective.

Your point of natural drift can also have an impact on how you follow Jesus. When you first believe in Jesus, you are made holy, which we've talked about. Just in case you need a reminder: God sees you as His holy child. Then, we are on the journey of living out that holiness and being transformed to be more like Jesus over time through sanctification. It is in this journey that

---

[1] C. S. Lewis, *Mere Christianity* (1952; repr. New York: HarperOne, 2009), 22.

our natural tendency to drift toward one extreme or the other will try to take us off course and hinder our progress.

The basic issue is based in achievement, but depending on your point of view, it fleshes itself out differently. If you drift toward the high extreme, then your temptation will be to approach your sanctification journey in your own power, believing that following Jesus is an act of the will and hard work more than a work of God in your life through the Holy Spirit. The Bible tells us differently. Philippians 2:13 says, "For it is God who is working in you both to will and to work according to his good purpose." Just as it is God working in you to bring you into His family, it is God working in you to bring you closer to Him in your lifestyle.

We see God's initiative and power in our sanctification again in 2 Peter 1:3: "His divine power has given us everything required for life and godliness through the knowledge of him who called us by his own glory and goodness." Notice the emphasis here is on Jesus. It is Jesus' power that has given you everything you need for life and godliness, for your sanctification journey. It is also through the knowledge of Jesus that this power comes to you. This concept should be familiar to you from chapter 2. You grow in your knowledge of Jesus through His Word, and as you grow in your knowledge of Jesus, His power grows in you to help you continue moving forward in your sanctification. If you naturally drift toward the high-view extreme, God's power in you is important for you to grasp, because in your own power, no matter how hard you try, you will always end up frustrated.

It is truly tragic when people strive so hard for the things of God and end up missing God Himself altogether. It happened to the religious elite Pharisees in the Bible, and I've seen it happen to more teenagers than I can count from my time in student ministry. It is amazing, though, to see a high-view person suddenly understand this concept and begin to shape their life around God's power rather than their own. My prayer for you in this journey is that God will use this moment to open your eyes to that truth.

If you drift toward the low-view extreme, then your issue is still connected to achievement. This may seem counterintuitive, but think about it this way: instead of thinking you can do it all in your own power, you are tempted to think you will never be able to do it. For you, the sanctification journey and becoming more like Jesus seems impossible because you see things through your personal failures. While some people may think they're so good they can do it on their own, you may be tempted to think you're so bad that not even God can do it for you. Your Christian life looks like a constant battle to become more like Jesus, only to have a moment of failure and lose all your progress.

As I said, I know this issue well. It's one that I've struggled with in the past and one that will likely try to trip me up again in the future. The same verses about God's power working in you that we looked at in the previous section still apply. It isn't up to you. God has given you everything you need for life, godliness, and to do His will. Do you remember the chart that we looked at in chapter 2? Did you notice how that line moving up and to the right, the one representing your sanctification journey, wasn't perfectly straight? There are jagged moments and drops in that line because there are going to be times of failure. We aren't perfect people, but in God's power—the same power that raised Jesus from the dead, by the way—the overall trajectory of our lives can move toward becoming like Jesus.

But, in those times of failure, you need to know how to respond. You need a way to fend off those attacks. In Ephesians 6, Paul talks about the armor of God. This is the spiritual armor that God gives us to be able to withstand the spiritual attacks that come our way. One of those pieces is the "sword of the Spirit—which is the word of God" (v. 17). The Word of God is a sword because it is to be used as both an offensive and defensive piece, just like you see swords throughout history being used. Your tendency to dwell on your failures to the point where they overtake you is a very real attack, but your Bible, the Scripture that you have learned and are learning, is your weapon against that attack.

You must arm yourself with God's Word, and I want to give you a place to start. Colossians 2:13–14 says, "And when you were dead in your trespasses and in the uncircumcision of your flesh, he made you alive with him and forgave us all our trespasses. He erased the certificate of debt, with its obligations, that was against us and opposed to us, and has taken it away by nailing it to the cross." Child of God, you are *forgiven*. You are forgiven of the sin in your life before you first believed in Jesus, you're forgiven for the sin you committed last night, you're forgiven of the sin you will commit next week, and you're forgiven of the sin you'll commit fifty years from now. Your sin has been erased and He has removed your sin from you "as far as the east is from the west" (Ps. 103:12). Your sin has been nailed to the cross and He has removed the guilt and shame that go along with it. He is not holding your failures against you. He is not angry with you and He hasn't turned His back on you, because through Jesus, there is nothing that can separate you from His love (Rom. 8:31–39). Your life isn't about success and failure anymore because Jesus was successful for you. Rest in the truth that you are valuable because you are created in His image, you are loved, you have been made holy, and you have been given everything you need through Jesus and His Word to live out that holiness right now.

## A Caution

Okay, now for the caution. It would be easy to walk away from this chapter thinking that your journey of sanctification just happens to you, because we've talked a lot about God's power in you, Him working in you, and His provision for you in your journey.

Those things are absolutely true, but it is also true that there are actions we must take. While we do naturally drift toward a certain view of ourselves, we don't naturally drift toward holiness. D. A. Carson, in his book *For the Love of God*, says, "People do not drift toward holiness. Apart from grace-driven effort, people do not gravitate toward godliness, prayer, obedience to Scripture, faith and delight in the Lord."[2]

Colossians 3 gives us a list of things that as believers we are to avoid. In verse 5, God tells us we are to "put to death what belongs to your earthly nature." The section goes on to say that we are to "put away" sin and "put on" the new self. There is a marriage here between God working in us through His power, providing the way for us to grow in sanctification, and us choosing to obey and follow Him. We have to walk in His power, not just sit in it, and it is much more than a moralistic pursuit of being "good." There is more to the concept of grace-driven effort than what we will cover here, as entire books have been devoted to the subject, but I do want to introduce it to you and encourage you to research it more.[3]

The first place I would point you is to Matt Chandler's book *Explicit Gospel*. In it, he says this on the subject:

> Grace-driven effort is violent. It is aggressive. The person who understands the gospel understands that, as a new creation, his spiritual nature is in opposition to sin now, and he seeks not just to weaken sin in his life but to outright destroy it. Out of love for Jesus, he wants sin starved to death, and he will hunt and pursue the death of every sin in his heart until he has achieved

---

[2] D. A. Carson, *For the Love of God*, Vol. 2 (Wheaton, IL: Crossway, 1999), 23.

[3] For further study, I recommend Sinclair Ferguson's *The Whole Christ*.

success. This is a very different pursuit than simply wanting to be good. It is the result of having
transferred one's affections to Jesus. When God's
love takes hold of us, it powerfully pushes out our
own love for other gods and frees our love to flow
back to him in true worship. And when we love
God, we obey him.[4]

As you can see, it is an intense action that we must take
against sin, but it is still in God's power, because of His love for
us, and out of a love for Him. The way we view ourselves—and
our natural tendency to drift to one extreme or the other—has
a direct impact on the way we see our relationship with Jesus.
Remember, you have the Holy Spirit in you. He is working to draw
you away from the unhealthy places you naturally drift in order to
move you closer to Jesus and His holiness.

We all come from different places, perspectives, and backgrounds that influence our Christian lives, but one thing we all
have in common is that we are in it together. God has placed His
Holy Spirit within us and is with us every step of the way, but
we are also meant to be on this sanctification journey together.
We are meant to love Jesus together, fight sin together, encourage each other, challenge each other, and love each other. Just as
important as understanding God's view of you and your view of
yourself is your view of the other people who are in the Christian
life with you.

Going to college can seem like your whole world is changing right
before you, and that's because it is. Everything you are familiar with
is taken away from you and replaced with the unknown. When I was
making that transition from high school and college, my parents were

---

[4] Matt Chandler, *Explicit Gospel* (Wheaton, IL: Crossway, 2012),
217–18.

also getting a divorce, we moved from one state to another, and I ended a relationship that I had put so much of my hope and identity into. Everything that I had thought made up who I was—my family, my home and my best friend—was suddenly taken away from me. I felt like I couldn't control a single thing in my life—that is, except what I ate. This spiraled into a severe eating disorder. It started off as anorexia, but soon led to bulimia when I lost control and immediately felt a flood of regret. I was just longing for control over one thing in my life, and I thought that this would surely satisfy my heart. But it soon led to the exactly opposite.

By the grace of God, I was surrounded at a school in Virginia called Liberty University by friends who chased after the heart of God with everything they had. These friends circled around me and taught me about what He says about my worth. They showed me that the safest and sweetest place to be is when I release control and give the Creator of the heavens and the earth full control over my life. Slowly but surely the Lord restored my heart and my thoughts; no longer did I want to strive to put my life together but my outlook changed to how can I give the Lord glory in the best possible way while I'm here on earth in this body that I am just renting for a little while. Does that mean that life will always be easy, sweet, and carefree? Not always. Does that mean that I know Jesus works all things out for His glory and my good? Always. You may be like the 20 percent of college students who struggle with an eating disorder at some point; so I would just love to encourage you: nothing feels better than releasing control over to the God of the universe. Is it a scary thing? Yes. Is it worth it? Absolutely.

—Camille Shepherd, Liberty University graduate; college girls associate from Cross Church college ministry in Fayetteville, Arkansas

# Part 3

# The Church

# Chapter 5

# The Church: What It Is and What It Does

BEING PART OF A church is an essential part of your college experience. There are statistics galore about the number of college students that leave the church during their college years, as well as arguments back and forth on the accuracy of the number. What we do know is that 70–80 percent of students who attended a church while in high school will not attend church for an extended period of time during their college years.[1]

Being part of a church isn't just an essential part of your college experience; it's an essential part of your relationship with God. The church plays an important role in your journey of sanctification, and to walk away from it will have a detrimental impact on your spiritual health.

Throughout this section, I want to help you understand what the church is, what the church is not, the role the church is meant to play in our world, and your role within the church.

There are few graduating high school seniors who truly value the church for what it is and what it is meant to accomplish. One of the places where this is most evident is when you and your family made your college visits. There is a high chance that you didn't attend a church, look for churches in the area, or meet with

---

[1] www.christianitytoday.com/edstetzer/2014/may/dropouts-and-disciples-how-many-students-are-really-leaving.html

any pastors from local churches while you were checking out the school where you would spend the next four-plus years of your life. Because of this, I want to make sure that you have an understanding of the church in general in the hope that your view of the church would grow to the place that it deserves in your life.

## Let's Define Our Terms

The best place to start is with a simple definition of the church: "the community of all true believers for all time" is a definition given by theologian Wayne Grudem.[2] It can also be described as those people "belonging to the Lord."[3] The word used in the New Testament for the church translates to the "called-out ones." At the very highest level of this definition, the Church is all of God's people—past, present, and future—who have been called out from the world and into His family.

When you first believe in Jesus, you become part of the Church. This is a simple statement; so simple, in fact, that you can miss its significance. As a part of God's family, His called-out ones, *you are connected to all believers around the world.* You have brothers and sisters in Christ across the globe. This isn't something you did; it's something God did when He saved you. He saved you into something—the Church. First Corinthians 12:13 puts it this way: "We were all baptized by one Spirit into one body." You are a part of the Church; it happened the moment you were saved.

There have been a few times when this truth has been especially impactful to me. One of them was in the Dominican Republic and one was in East Asia. In both of these instances I

---

[2] Wayne Grudem, *Systematic Theology* (Grand Rapids, MI: Zondervan, 1994), 853.

[3] Millard J. Erickson, *Christian Theology*, 2nd ed. (Grand Rapids, MI: 1998), 1040.

was with missionaries and local believers within the communities where we were traveling. Our group had the opportunity to worship with these local believers. To be able to stand next to other believers who were praying and worshipping in their native languages while I did the same in mine was an amazing experience.

I've never felt more welcomed than I felt walking into believers' homes in East Asia. We were treated like family even though we had never met and will probably never see each other again, all because we shared a belief in Jesus.

There are believers all over the world that you are connected to because you are part of God's Church.

Most often though, when we think about the church we think about it in terms of its local expression. If you want to do some additional study on the church, spend some time reading the book of Acts. There, you will find God beginning to gather His people together, and it will give you a great picture of how followers of Jesus first began meeting together and many of the hardships and joys that they faced in the earliest years together.[4]

In the New Testament, we see examples of local groups of Christians meeting together as churches. In that time, some met in homes (Rom. 16:5; Col. 4:15), while some met in groups larger than what a home could hold. Many of Paul's writings in the New Testament were written to groups of believers from a specific region and were circulated and read aloud in places where the local believers were gathering together. We even see Paul giving instructions about church meetings in 1 Corinthians 14. These local gatherings of believers have multiplied throughout generations and are still active all over the world today as groups

---

[4] Other resources to consider are *What Is a Healthy Church?* by Mark Dever, *What Is a Healthy Church Member?* by Thabiti Anyabwile, *Church Membership* by Jonathan Leeman, *Sojourners and Strangers* by Gregg Allison, and *Life Together* by Dietrich Bonhoeffer.

of believers, large and small, gather to be with one another in fellowship and to worship God.

This brings us to an important question: What makes a gathering of believers a church? Is it safe to say that any gathering of believers can be considered a church? While all believers are part of the universal Church, to function as a church in a local expression there are a couple of things that have to be present.

In a meeting of believers that took place in 1530, there was a document created called the Augsburg Confession. In this confession, the church was defined as "the congregation of saints in which the gospel is rightly taught and the Sacraments rightly administered" (Article 7). The first piece of this statement refers to the gospel being rightly taught, and is the most important thing to look for when you are looking for a church to join. There are many warped views of the gospel in our culture, so you must be in the practice of checking everything you hear (and read, for that matter) with God's Word. We spent the first chapter of this book walking through the gospel so that you would have an understanding for yourself, but also so that you can learn to spot warped gospels as you hear them.

A church that fully and rightly preaches the gospel will see Scripture alone as our highest authority, will teach that salvation comes only through faith in Jesus and only by God's grace, that Jesus alone is our Savior and the only way to the Father, and that we live for God's glory alone. This list of five things is known as the "Five Solas," and they have been foundational pillars of the Christian church from the time of Scripture. Thankfully, these five truths were reclaimed in the sixteenth century and have been passed on to us today.

Our definition from earlier also mentioned administration of the sacraments. This refers to baptism and the Lord's Supper. Baptism that took place in the New Testament was done by immersing someone in water, and it was done after someone placed their faith in Jesus. Baptism doesn't bring salvation; it is a visible act whereby a person gives testimony that he or she has begun following Jesus. It is also an act of obedience, as baptism was commanded by Jesus (Matt. 28:19) and the apostles (Acts 2:38) and seen after Peter preaches in Acts 2:41, after Philip preached in Acts 8:12, and after an Ethiopian begins following Jesus in Acts 8:36. Baptism is also referred to as common practice by Paul in Romans 6:3–4 and Colossians 2:12.

Baptism is the public identifier that someone is entering into *the* Church, as well as becoming part of *a* church. Because of this, for a group of believers who are gathering together to truly be a church, there must be a practice of baptizing new believers.

The other sacrament that is used as an identifier for a church truly being a church is the Lord's Supper. The Lord's Supper is practiced throughout a person's life as a part of a church in order to remember and celebrate Jesus' actions for us in the gospel. Some churches observe it more than others, and there isn't a strict guideline given for how often it should be done, only that it is to be done in remembrance of Jesus (1 Cor. 11:23–25). Observing the Lord's Supper is a worshipful action that we get to take part in to keep our minds focused on the gospel and to give evidence that we continue to follow Jesus.

The combination of these three things: preaching of the gospel, baptism, and the Lord's Supper, have been understood as the guidelines for what defines a church for hundreds of years, and have been affirmed continually even today. By defining what the church is, we should be able to deduce what the church is not—but I still want to mention a couple of things here.

More than likely, there will be several Christian groups that meet on campus at your school. There will be some that do great things in the community and around the world, as well as faithfully teach the Bible. As good as these organizations are, being involved in one of them is different than being involved in a local church. A group like this may faithfully teach the Word, but doesn't observe baptism and the Lord's Supper. If those things aren't happening, then it isn't a church. In the same way, if the full gospel isn't faithfully and consistently being preached, then it isn't a church.

Please understand, I'm not speaking out against these organizations or saying you shouldn't be involved in one. Many of them are helpful for countless numbers of college students. What I am saying is they shouldn't be seen as a church or as a replacement for one. The choice to replace being part of a church with some other organization is dangerous because it takes you out of experiencing the purposes of the church with other people who belong to the church.

Not being part of a church also goes against a scriptural command. In Hebrews 10:24–25, the Bible says, "And let us watch out for one another to provoke love and good works, not neglecting to gather together, as some are in the habit of doing, but encouraging each other, and all the more as you see the day approaching." This verse is part of a larger section where the writer is encouraging believers toward godliness, and it is within that context that we see the command for us to not neglect gathering together—specifically, the writer of Hebrews is talking about gathering together in a local church.

You can also see that even in the time of the Bible there was a group of people whose habit was apparently to neglect being part of the church. This isn't a new thing, but it is one thing the Bible specifically addresses.

As a believer in Jesus, you need to be part of a church for your own spiritual health and obedience. This "gathering together" as the church was so important to the lives of the early believers that they devoted themselves to meeting together at the temple daily (Acts 2:46). At this point, it's important that you understand that the church was not man's idea. Throughout the

Bible—Old Testament included—we see a pattern of God gathering His people together. Then when Jesus entered the world, the formation of the church into what it would be in the future began to take shape. In Matthew 16:18, Jesus is having a conversation with Peter and He tells Peter that the church would be built on the confession of Jesus as Lord as the rock, or foundation, of the church. The church as we know it began with Jesus, and the Bible uses similar language referring to Jesus as the "foundation" of the church in 1 Corinthians 3:11, Ephesians 2:20, and 1 Peter 2.

The church was not man's idea; it was God's. He began it with Jesus; it was passed down to the apostles, then to others, and others, and still others, until it has come to us today. Has it been perfect throughout these years? No, because imperfect people have been involved. What we do see throughout church history, however, is a faithful God who has consistently raised up leaders to guide people back to Him and help the church carry out His mission on earth.

## The Great Commission

Since the church was God's idea, He decides its purpose. This purpose is the reason we're still here—the reason God doesn't immediately take us into heaven when we're saved. Primarily, this purpose is to spread the gospel to the ends of the earth.

You will see in Acts that the very first church began to explode and multiply quickly in number because of the gospel being shared and people believing in Jesus. Sharing the gospel story is central to the function of the church. In Matthew 28:19, Jesus hands over the reins of ministry to the disciples and gives them this command: "Go, therefore, and make disciples of all nations, baptizing them in the name of the Father, and of the Son, and of the Holy Spirit." Shortly after this moment, Jesus returned to heaven, and the disciples were left to abandon the cause or to follow in obedience. We see the choice that they made begin to unfold throughout the book of Acts, as they eagerly spread the gospel message in spite of intense persecution. Ten of the original twelve disciples were killed because of their faith in Jesus and their work spreading His story wherever they went. These men died for their faith, many have died for their faith from that time until today, and still others continue to die for their faith in our world right now because of their willingness to obey Jesus' command to share the gospel message.

As you consider churches in your area to be part of throughout your college experience, make sure to choose one that faithfully preaches the gospel of Jesus and works to carry that gospel to the ends of the earth.

If you continue to look at Jesus' parting words to His disciples in Matthew 28, you will see that it doesn't stop with the command to baptize. Here is what He says in verse 20: "teaching them to observe everything I have commanded you. And remember, I am with you always, to the end of the age." Jesus' command for the church to teach people how to follow Him is part of the very same command for the church to evangelize. These two tasks can't be separated; the church must engage in both at equal levels. A church that really gets this command will equip you to share the gospel and will teach you how to know and obey God, and how to teach others to know and obey God. A church that is faithful in the role of teaching will also be a pillar of truth within the community in which it exists. It will stand for truth without fear, even in a culture that doesn't want to hear it, and it will do so with a spirit of love and grace, rather than condemnation.

Being a pillar of truth doesn't mean that we go out of our way to offend people or turn the Bible into a hammer that we repeatedly use to club people so we can feel good. That approach is anti-Jesus, as we see Jesus' purpose for coming to earth in John 3:17: "For God did not send his Son into the world to condemn the world, but to save the world through him." Jesus came to speak the truth in order that people would be saved, not as a way to condemn people. A church that is a pillar of truth in the community will handle this obligation in the same way.

## Worship

As the church engages in evangelism and teaching (both of these put together is called discipleship), people will be drawn to worship God, which is another significant role of the church.

God's people have been worshipping Him from the beginning. Throughout the Old Testament, altars were built and sacrifices were made in order to worship God. The Psalms are a living testimony of God's desire for His people to worship Him. A general definition of worship is "the activity of glorifying God in his presence with our voices and hearts."[5]

Worship is most often thought of as singing, but we also worship God through the teaching and hearing of His Word corporately, privately as we pray and read His Word, and even through our choices to obey and live for Him along our journey of sanctification. Colossians 3:16–17 speaks to these different forms of worship: "Let the word of Christ dwell richly among you, in all wisdom teaching and admonishing one another through psalms, hymns, and spiritual songs, singing to God with gratitude in your hearts. And whatever you do, in word or deed, do everything in the name of the Lord Jesus, giving thanks to God the Father through him."

The church is called to provide opportunities for its people to gather together and worship God. It is also called to equip them to live a life that brings glory to God in all things. We see this again in Romans 12:1: "Therefore, brothers and sisters, in view of the

---

[5] Wayne Grudem, *Systematic Theology* (Grand Rapids, MI: Zondervan, 1994), 1003.

mercies of God, I urge you to present your bodies as a living sacrifice, holy and pleasing to God; this is your true worship." What, according to that verse, is worship? It is a response to the mercy of God whereby we totally devote ourselves to Him in everything we do. A healthy, gospel-centered church will gather together to worship corporately, and it will send its members out to worship individually.

## Meeting Needs

The final role of the church that I want to mention is the church's responsibility of meeting the needs of people. James 1:27 clearly states that God's people are to "look after" orphans and widows, and Hebrews 13:3 instructs us to "remember those in prison, as though you were in prison with them, and the mistreated, as though you yourselves were suffering bodily." In Acts 6:1–7, we see two more evidences of the ministry and need-meeting role of the church. This section mentions widows again and also adds that there is a daily distribution taking place. The people of the church would come to the church in order to get supplies, like food and clothing, so that their basic needs would be met. In Acts 2:44–45 and 4:32 we see generosity overflowing within the church as people sold possessions and property, bringing the money earned to the apostles so that it could be distributed to people who were in need.

God's church is a generous, giving church that meets the needs of people.

Being part of a church is necessary for you to continue growing in your journey of sanctification. Just like there are specific roles that the church plays in the world, there are specific roles for you as part of a local church. That is where we turn next.

## Chapter 6

# Your Role in the Church

**HAVE YOU EVER THOUGHT** of yourself as an essential part of the church? Have you ever thought that the church wouldn't function as effectively without you?

The average church member doesn't think about church that way. For the majority of Christians, church is treated like any other organization that offers a consumable good or service. People show up a few times per month, attend a worship service, consume the music and the sermon (skipping the announcements if they can), and then go on about the rest of their day with little to no change or impact having been made at all. This can be true even in churches that are fulfilling their roles in evangelism, teaching, worship, and ministry.

This happens because the people *of* the church rarely embrace their roles *in* the church. Because our society trains us to think the pastors and staff are the professionals doing the work of the ministry, we see our role as that of consumer. After all, if there is a paid professional in the church, why does the average person sitting in the crowd need to do anything?

This mind-set causes churches to become less effective in their roles. The church cannot function without the people. Yes, the church was God's idea and established by Jesus, but the design that God put in place is that His people would cause the church to function and be effective. People are an essential part of the church, because people are the church. The church is not a building or a location, it is the group of believers that meets together that makes up the church. And for a church to truly function the way it was designed, the people of God need to embrace their own roles within it. This is true for you even if you are only going to be in that community for four years during college. The church needs you, and you need it.

I began serving in my church at the beginning of my junior year, and it was by accident. My schedule at that time was very busy and so I had very few breaks, but I would always be sure to take a break to attend my church's Wednesday night college service. I had a very small window of time to get dinner after class on Wednesdays, so I would have to get food and then take it to the church and eat it outside before going in for the service. Every time I would arrive, people would joke around and laugh because I was eating dinner on the sidewalk, but I began to get to know the other students who served the church because they'd always talk to me. As we talked I would help them out by setting up tables or extra chairs and just doing anything that I was asked to do. As I continued to serve each week, I began to realize how much joy serving my fellow students brought me and how it laid a foundation for me to form relationships with everyone that came through the doors.

I was then given more responsibility by our pastor and the other leaders in our church, which increased my area of influence while also encouraging me to serve more. Throughout all of this time my schedule was still just as busy as before—I was the vice president of my fraternity, I was studying or doing homework every night, and I was leading a weekly Bible study group. I learned that even though I wasn't required to serve the church every week, it was a time that God would reveal biblical truths to me. Even though it seemed like I could've taken those extra hours to catch up on sleep or homework, I knew that the Lord was going to use me in some way.

Mark 10:43–45 says, "But it is not so among you. On the contrary, whoever wants to become great among you will be your servant, and whoever wants to be first among you will be a slave to all. For even the Son of Man did not come to be served, but to serve, and to give his life as a ransom for many." In this passage Jesus is telling His disciples about the importance of serving others, and if they put the needs of others before their own they will be made great. In the same way, the Lord has taught me so many things through time spent serving the church and He has strengthened me in multiple areas of my life.

—Joe Massey, vice president of Beta Upsilon Chi at the University of Arkansas; senior medical student

## The Church: A Body

The Bible uses the example of a human body to illustrate the interdependence that exists between the people of the church and the church fulfilling its purpose. In 1 Corinthians 12:12–27, Paul is writing to a group of Christians and explaining this relationship. He begins by saying, "For just as the body is one and has many parts, and all the parts of that body, though many, are one body—so also is Christ." He goes on to talk about different body parts and how silly it would be for a foot to say, "I'm not part of the body," or for another part to say, "because I'm not an eye, I don't belong to the body" (v. 16). He makes the case that each part of the human body has a specific function that is vital to the body's overall health. He asks, "If the whole body were an eye, where would the hearing be? If the whole body were an ear, where would the sense of smell be? But as it is, God has arranged each one of the parts in the body just as he wanted" (vv. 17–18). God made us to fit together like a body so that when we are in the church together there would "be no division in the body, but that the members would have the same concern for each other" (v. 25). Paul ends this part with the affirmation that the people of God are all part of the "body of Christ" (v. 27).

You already know from what you have studied in science classes that the individual parts of the body are completely interdependent upon each other to function correctly. When one part is damaged or broken, the rest of the body is less effective. The body is used as an illustration in this passage to reinforce the truth that each person in the church is just as important as every other person. There is no favoritism, gift, or position that is more honorable than another. Each person is needed for the body to function correctly.

This passage also makes clear that we are to suffer and celebrate alongside each other as part of the church. Being part of a church means that you are so connected to others in the church that you are able to actually do these things, that you know when someone else is struggling so that you can support them and so that other people can support you during those same times. When we approach the church with a consumer's mind-set, we will never get to the place that Paul describes here.

There's another place where the illustration of the body is used to describe the church, again written by Paul, found in Ephesians 4. Because it is the same writer and the same topic, you will see some similarities here, but with a little bit of a different twist. Verses 15–16 say, "But speaking the truth in love, let us grow in every way into him who is the head—Christ. From him the whole body, fitted and knit together by every supporting ligament, promotes the growth of the body for building up itself in love by the proper working of each individual part." One difference in this passage from the other one is that Christ is identified as the head of the body.

To understand the importance of this small phrase, think about your head and its role in your body. It's the control center. Without the head, nothing else functions. We can survive—although less than optimally—without an ear or a hand or a toe. But we can't survive without our head.

The head is the place of authority and power over the rest of the body. Jesus as the head means that each person who is part of the body is to submit to Him. This kind of authority or "headship" is clearly seen in Galatians 2:20: "and I no longer live, but Christ lives in me. The life I now live in the body, I live by faith in the Son of God, who loved me and gave himself for me."

As we talked about earlier in the book, the power to live like Jesus comes from Jesus. Your journey of sanctification is a personal one first, between you and God through Christ, and now I hope you are beginning to see that your sanctification journey is also connected to other believers. We are all fitted and knit together as body parts and supporting ligaments so that we can accomplish the purpose of the body being built up in love. Growth comes from Jesus as the head, and as we grow individually, we will also grow together as the body of Christ. As I grow in my obedience to Him and my faith increases, it serves as a strengthening influence for the obedience and faith of others in my church to grow along with me. It has the same effect on me when other believers around me are growing.

Glance back at the very last part of the Ephesians 4 passage: "by the proper working of each individual part" (v. 16). The proper working of each individual person within the church is what it takes to be built up in love, to grow in Christ, to move forward on our journey of sanctification, and for the church to fulfill its role in the world. God has made all of us beautifully diverse in our backgrounds, experiences, talents, and abilities. When you are part of a church, you bring all of these things with you, and the rest of the church benefits from your involvement. You also benefit from the backgrounds, experiences, talents, and abilities of the other believers within the church. When you choose to not be involved in a church or to think of the church with a consumer's mind-set, you weaken both the church and your own journey of sanctification. If you aren't currently part of a church, then you need to make the decision to find one. If you are part of one now and you are just showing up, sitting, observing, and leaving, then you need to become more involved. The church needs you, and you need the church.

## Join a Small Group

One of the most important ways to get more involved in a church is to be part of a small group. The Christian life is meant to be lived in community with other believers. This is what we see in the New Testament—groups of believers eating, fellowshipping, and caring for each other. Being part of a small group is the best way to truly get to know a group of people well enough to suffer and celebrate with them, as we saw in 1 Corinthians 12, and to build each other up in love, as we saw in Ephesians 4.

Did you ever play the game Red Rover when you were a kid? If so, then the phrase, "Red Rover, Red Rover, send Billy right over," is bringing a flood of memories to you from your childhood. Even now, you are picturing the kid—maybe it was you—who was repeatedly clotheslined as he or she tried to break the chain of arms at the other end of the field. Red Rover is one of those classic school yard games. Sadly, it is also a game that has decreased in popularity due to fear of concussion and the self-esteem degradation of being picked as the weakest person in the line to be "sent over." Ahh, what a great game . . .

As with any game, strategies are developed over time to help you win. For Red Rover, teams began to learn that the way to keep an opposing team member from breaking through the line, regardless of their size and strength, was to treat your own line like it is elastic. You don't win Red Rover by trying to grip each other's wrists and hands as tightly as you can. You win when the entire line collapses at the point of attack and bends with the two people who have been picked out as the target. Red Rover, at its core, is a game about community, not about having the strongest person on your team.

Let me start off by saying that you are EXACTLY where you are supposed to be. Even if it all feels wrong, be encouraged because our feelings are unreliable. I trust that the Lord has gone before you. He has made a way for you and His plans are perfect and divine. He is directing you in His way, He is closing doors and opening others so that you end up right where He wants you. Because He is going to use you, He is going to do incredible things in and through you. Let Him prepare you and use you and let Him be God.

One thing I remember from freshman year of college is learning how self-centered I am. In my flesh, my thoughts are about me, my actions are about me, my decisions are about me. It doesn't have to be that way for you. I know you have all the freedom in the world now, but take that freedom and invest in things bigger than yourself. Invest in community, invest in your roommate (even if it was potluck and you think you'll never be friends, I promise that it wasn't by accident), invest in the people in your classes, invest in school, invest in organizations, invest in a church—go serve, get plugged in, join a small group. Invest in your friends from high school—they know you AND love you, if you feel like no one does in your new college circle. Do not invest in partying and drinking and all the things of the world. I wish you could hear me when I tell you it's not worth it. It's not worth the shame, it's not worth the emptiness, it's not worth the pain. It's just not worth it. I know the weird feeling that comes with your freshman year of college. You are constantly surrounded by people, but have never felt so lonely. I get it. It doesn't make sense, and it hurts, but learn how to be alone—remember to be still, spend time with just you and Jesus, and go call your mom and your best friend from home.

—Hayley Quigley

We can learn a lot from this game and from the strategy that it takes to win. In order for you to truly grow in your faith, to be in a place where transformation is most likely to occur, you need to be connected to a small group. Yes, you can grow in obedience to God in a number of different environments, but a small group of believers whom you get to know and walk through life with is the best environment for transformation. When you are in a small group with other believers, you have the benefit of learning from them, their mistakes, and what they are learning along their journey. The others can also benefit from you in this same way. You can share each other's hurts and celebrate each other's victories.

I don't mean to bring the mood down with this, but the truth is, you will experience hardship this year. You will experience some kind of struggle as you try to fix your eyes on Jesus. The group of people that you experience life with, that you link arms with, will be the ones who bend and collapse around you when you enter into difficult times. They are the people the Lord will use to make sure the line doesn't break with the force of the attack.

Being part of this community gives you an opportunity to link arms with other believers and live out the partnership in the gospel that you are meant to have. Philippians 1:3–6 puts it like this:

> I give thanks to my God for every remembrance of you, always praying with joy for all of you in my every prayer, because of your partnership in the gospel from the first day until now. I am sure of this, that he who started a good work in you will carry it on to completion until the day of Christ Jesus.

In this passage we see one of the great promises of God, made to us as His children: God will finish the good work He started in us. He is going to make sure that you complete your journey of sanctification. You will be able to finish because God is with you and because He wants to place people around you to partner with you in the gospel. It is through this partnership with others that God is going to move you further along in your journey. Because of this, your involvement in a small group is essential to your continual growth in your faith.

Being part of a small group gives you support in the times you need it, helps you to grow in your journey of sanctification, and will help to keep you from sin. I mentioned a quote from Dietrich Bonhoeffer earlier in the book that is good for us to be reminded of here: "Sin demands to have a man by himself." When you aren't involved in a church and aren't walking closely with a group of believers, you are more susceptible to sin. You are more likely to experience temptation, and you are more likely to give in to that temptation. Part of this is simply because there's a lack of accountability. With no one around to help you stay strong in temptation or to point out when you are living in sin, your tendency will be to continue to spiral downward into sins that you struggle to avoid.

This means that when you are living life with a group of people, you will also be vulnerable with them, letting them into your life. This is where things get difficult and it's also where most people bail out of community. In general, we have a great fear of being truly known, with all of our imperfections and failures. In this fear, we remove ourselves from the community that God has designed to help us in those imperfections and failures.

Maybe this is a moment that you need to return to the identity section of this book for a quick reminder of who you are as God's child. Jesus makes you perfect in God's sight, and you are forgiven of all those things that you hide away from people, hoping that they will never find out. You are made clean. And what you will come to find is that other people have a fear of vulnerability as well—but that isn't the most important thing that you have in common. What brings you together with others in community and allows you to break through the barriers to vulnerability is the same as what teaches you and moves you along in your individual journey: the Holy Spirit. As He works in your life and in the lives of those around you, you will be bound closer together, and your relationships will begin to be shaped by His sanctifying work, leading you to relate to each other in grace, mercy, and compassion.

Being part of a small group isn't just a good idea; it is a God-designed pathway for you to grow closer to Him. To step out of community is to step out of discipleship.

# Chapter 7

# Discipleship and Disciple-Making

**I KNOW THAT AS** a college student you want to be around other college students. Your high school days are over and you desire to quickly move to more mature things (or at least things that seem more mature). You are also in this strange middle ground where, if you're absolutely honest with yourself, you don't quite feel like an adult, so it doesn't make sense for you to spend a lot of time with "adults" or older people that you don't have anything in common with.

Add these two colliding desires—eagerness to leave youth behind and not yet feeling like an adult—to a dorm living situation, and the natural result is an environment where college students are only around other college students. There's no real connection with anyone outside your generation unless you purposefully seek it out, and many do not.

This is another reason why the church shouldn't be replaced with a Christian organization or some type of collegiate ministry that is not connected to a church. Generational discipleship is a clear biblical principle and it is something that most college students miss because of a lack of church involvement, a replacement of the church for some other ministry, or plain old neglect. The church (local gathering of believers) is the way that God designed for you to be connected to other generations of believers. It isn't healthy for you to only be with other college students, especially in a spiritual environment. In your journey of sanctification, you can learn through personal experience only or you can learn through personal experience plus the experiences of others. People who have been on their own journey for longer than you can offer you a perspective that is impossible for you to see at this point in your life. Learning from them, their hardships, struggles, and victories, can be a great encouragement and help to you in your own journey. As they've lived with Jesus, their view of God has grown, and listening to their stories of God's faithfulness can grow your view of Him as well.

Psalm 145:4 talks about this very thing: "One generation will declare your works to the next and will proclaim your mighty acts." As someone who is in one of the most critical seasons of your life, you need to put yourself in a place where you are regularly hearing about the great works of God from an older generation.

Being connected to older generations can also help you avoid sin. Take a look at 1 Corinthians 10:13, "No temptation has come upon you except what is common to humanity. But God is faithful; he will not allow you to be tempted beyond what you are able, but with the temptation he will also provide a way out so that you may be able to bear it." The first thing I want you to see from this passage is that all temptation is common to humanity. What you are dealing with isn't something that is isolated to you. It may be something that is causing you deep shame and fear because you think you're alone in that struggle, but you aren't alone. The longer I walk with Jesus the more I am convinced that isolation is one of the major strategies of the enemy. We've mentioned it a couple of times in the book already, but I feel like it needs to be mentioned again in the hopes that repetition helps it to take root in your heart. You are not alone because the Holy Spirit is with you, and you aren't meant to be separated from other people because God has provided the church for believers to be able to walk through life together. Additionally, you shouldn't be isolated to your own generation, because there is far too much to learn than you can glean from your peers.

There are others that have walked through what you are dealing with right now. There are people further along in their sanctification journey that have fallen where you just fell or where you are about to fall. They have scars, bumps, and bruises that you can avoid by being connected to them and learning from what God has taught them along the way.

## Spiritual DNA

My dad is one of the godliest men I know. He was forty-nine years old when I was born, so my childhood and my relationship with my dad were a little different than most of the kids I knew. He was a high school counselor in California for the first thirteen years of my life, and has been a minister on staff at a church for the last twenty-five years. He currently serves as a prison chaplain in his hometown. I could point to a lot of things that have stood out to me over the years about my dad, but I think one thing rises above them all—how he lived out the biblical principle of generational discipleship.

My dad has always given his life to help younger men in their faith. When I was in elementary school there was one in particular who became like a brother to me because he was around so much. Some of the fondest memories of my childhood are when he would join my dad and me on fishing trips each year for the opening day of trout season in the California mountains. He is still a friend of the family.

What I didn't understand then is that this was all very intentional on my dad's part. He wasn't just being nice; he was engaging in generational discipleship to share what the Lord had taught him in the hope that it would impact the life of someone younger. This was the pattern that my dad has followed for as long as I can remember. Even now as I write this chapter, my dad is meeting with several guys, from high school age to men in their forties—men who have grown up in church, other ministers, ex-convicts, and current prisoners—all with the purpose of teaching them what God has taught him through the years. A desire for these relationships is hardwired into his DNA.

It's hardwired into your DNA as well. Maybe not the physical DNA, but definitely the DNA of your new identity in Christ. You are meant to be in this kind of mentoring relationship, to seek out wise older men or women and learn from their walk with the Lord.

Our verse from 1 Corinthians said that we would never be tempted beyond what we were able to avoid and that we would always have a way out. What if the way out that God has provided is found in the experiences of another believer? What if your way out of the temptation that is attacking you so aggressively is to learn from an older, wiser believer how they were able to fight against that same sin? I think we read this verse and we think that in each and every temptation there is a way out right there in the moment—and certainly that is the case at times. But I think the progressive nature of sin puts us into a place where the way out of temptation actually happens long before the point where we fall. There are a series of decisions, "little sins," that set us up for something we never thought we would struggle with or fall to. "Sin will take you farther than you want to go, keep you longer than you want to stay, and cost you more than you want to pay" is a statement that I've heard throughout my life. I'm not sure who said it originally, but it still rings true.

Generational discipleship and learning from those in the church who have lived longer and learned more than we have will provide us an off-ramp, a way out of sin that could otherwise cause significant damage to us later in life.

There are two more verses in the book of Proverbs that I want to bring to your attention on this topic. First, Proverbs 13:20 says, "The one who walks with the wise will become wise, but a companion of fools will suffer harm." I want to be clear that just because someone is older doesn't necessarily make them the "wise" people in this verse. When you think about someone, or a few people, to mentor or "disciple" you, they need to be people who are actively seeking the Lord in their own lives. Throughout your college experience you will have plenty of opportunity to be the companion of fools. Those are the easy relationships to have, which is why so many college students settle for them. It takes effort and often sacrifice to find wise people to walk with. You have to give up some things in order to make time for this kind of relationship.

To be clear, there are wise college students that you can find and walk through life with. I'm not advocating you spend all of your time with older people. Your small group community that we talked about in the last chapter is the perfect place to walk with wise people who are your peers. You need those relationships just as much as you need relationships with generations who have gone before you. But the truth remains that the collective wisdom of your group of college friends is not the same as the collective wisdom of the people who have been on their sanctification journey thirty or forty-plus years more than you.

The second verse is from Proverbs 27:17, and it says, "Iron sharpens iron, and one person sharpens another." This is a passage that can apply to both your peer discipleship relationships and the relationships that you have with older believers. The picture here of "sharpening another" literally means to "sharpen the face of another." Do you want to know how you can tell if you are walking (living life) alongside wise people? There will be a visible difference in you as a result of your time with them. They will help you grow in becoming more like Jesus.

Iron sharpening iron is not an easy thing. In fact, if you were to take two equal iron swords and bang them together over and over, they would not sharpen each other—they would grow more dull. But if you take an iron-sharpening device, a file of some kind, and an iron sword, you can run the file down the edges of the sword and it will sharpen it. In a sharpening process one thing always dominates and the other thing always gives in. The process isn't easy. When a sword is sharpened, it always gives up something from itself; it gives up a little bit of itself in order to more effectively accomplish its purpose.

When we think about this verse in the context of discipleship, there are two parts: a file and a sword. There will be seasons in your life when you serve as the file and seasons when you are the sword. There needs to be someone or a group of people in your life willing to file away your edges, to challenge you to give up something that is holding you back in your journey of sanctification.

The other part of this discipleship process is that you become the file for someone else, or a group of people. This same peer group that you are walking through this season of life with is the starting place for that as you all sharpen each other, which I hope is helping you see why being part of a small group community through your church is so important. There is also a great opportunity for you to find someone younger than you to begin a discipling relationship with. This is another place where the church needs you.

There is a common misconception that it is the job of the paid church staff to do all the work of the church—including discipling. This misconception is leading to church consumerism and is hurting the American church more and more. The true role of the staff is to help equip people like you to be both a file and a sword in the lives of other believers. Ephesians 4:11–12 drives this point home: "And he himself gave some to be apostles, some prophets, some evangelists, some pastors and teachers, equipping the saints for the work of the ministry, to build up the body of Christ." In these verses the saints that the church leaders are supposed to be training up so that the work of the ministry can be done are ordinary church members. You, as a member of a local church, are essential to the church fulfilling its role, and you can always spot a great church by the number of people it has serving in its various ministries.

According to this passage, when the people of the church are doing the ministry of the church, something amazing happens: the body of Christ is built up. As you know from the previous chapter, you are part of the body of Christ with other believers. The testimony of this passage is that as the people in the church serve in the church they all grow together and become more mature in their faith. I hope you are beginning to see the beautiful interdependent relationship that exists between the church, its people, and how they grow together along the journey of sanctification.

## Disciple-Making: The Great Commission

In Matthew 28:19–20, we read that Jesus commanded the disciples to go and make more disciples, to baptize them, and to teach them. We also talked about how God gave this mission of going to make disciples to His church, and the church has embraced that mission through the years until it has reached our time today. Now here you sit as a follower of Jesus and the command rests with you to go and make disciples.

The church has been given the mission, and there are tasks that the church has in our culture today (evangelism, teaching, worship, meeting needs generously), but the church can't accomplish them unless ordinary Christians live them out. We talked earlier about the global church and the local church—your role in the global church is to be part of a local church in order to help it accomplish God's mission in the world. You must be someone who is involved personally in evangelism, teaching, worship, and generously meeting people's needs. Just sitting in a church and consuming isn't good enough and it isn't your calling as a follower of Jesus. Your calling is to go make other disciples, and your college years are set up perfectly for you to both be in a discipling relationship with an older wiser believer and to pour your life into someone else to help them along their journey.

The college experience can be so much more than a life of experimentation, foolishness, and regret. Choose to follow Jesus, to walk your journey of sanctification, to be in biblical community, and to make disciples. This is the kind of college experience that impacts the lives of others and brings you to a place of abundance and joy.

# Part 4

# Pitfalls and How to Avoid Them

## Chapter 8

# What Is Wisdom?

**COLLEGE IS FILLED WITH** opportunities, freedom, decisions, challenges, and, if you'll allow it, growth. Being proactive, looking ahead, and being somewhat prepared with what you will be faced with can be a game changer for you.

If I could pinpoint one word of advice to you as you experience the college years, it would be to not only have wisdom but also know how to apply wisdom to your life. Wisdom will be what will keep you from falling into the devastating pitfalls of the "college experience." I know that is easy to say, but what, exactly, does it mean? What is wisdom? How do I apply wisdom to my life? How do I gain wisdom? In this chapter we're going to look at what God's Word has to say about wisdom and how to apply it to your life as a college student.

## The Beginning of Wisdom

Proverbs 9:10 is clear when it says, "The fear of the LORD is the beginning of wisdom, and the knowledge of the Holy One is understanding." The foundation for wisdom in our lives begins with a fear of the Lord. The fear of the Lord that Proverbs speaks of here is not being afraid of the Lord, as if He's going to strike you with a lightning bolt. A fear of the Lord is a deep love and respect for God and for His Word. We are to fear the Lord as we would a parent or guardian—those who are placed over us in authority to guide, protect, and discipline us for our own good. God is that authority. His rules and precepts for us to live by are not those of a hateful dictator but those of a caring Father who disciplines those He loves. They are for our protection and benefit. This is foundational for us to understand wisdom. When we fear the Lord and live with a holy, reverent fear of who God is, it changes everything!

This passage in Proverbs clearly tells us that knowledge of the Holy One results in good judgment, and fear of the Lord is the foundation of wisdom. Do you have a holy "fear" of the Lord? If not, ask Him to help you recognize how to continually live with awe and reverence of who He is in light of who you are.

"The college experience" is used by most to recollect a crazy, wild, fun, "free" season of life. For many students, the college experience is all about surviving and just making it through four years with no rules, regulations, or boundaries, all while justifying their questionable life choices by at least maintaining the GPA required to keep their scholarships and appease their parents and professors. Don't mistake your newfound "freedom" as an opportunity to live without any boundaries. That will always end up in mistakes, sin, and heartache, which ultimately leads to baggage that you could potentially carry with you for the rest of your life.

Let me introduce you to "Sarah." Sarah attends a public university in the traditional college town. As a college freshman, Sarah quickly discovered this new college town was full of unlimited freedom, parties, new people, and new experiences. Walking into this type of new environment you must understand and grasp what wisdom is; if you lack it, you will make unwise choices that could negatively impact your future

Sarah ended up making some unwise choices her freshman year which resulted in a sexual relationship in which she became pregnant. Not knowing what to do or who to turn to, she decided to take matters into her own hands. Worldly wisdom leads to making ungodly decisions, while godly wisdom leads to decisions that honor God. Sarah ended up following what cultural wisdom advised her to do instead of seeking godly advice and counsel, and as a result, she terminated her pregnancy.

You see, Sarah was a good girl. She grew up in a good home with loving parents, attended church periodically throughout high school, and was involved off and on in her student ministry. Although she attended church growing up, she didn't have a personal relationship with Jesus Christ, which resulted in falling into the temptations of the world. She found herself engulfed in the pitfall of the "college experience" of boys, parties, sex, and alcohol right out of the gate.

Godly wisdom leads to godly living; but worldly wisdom will lead to ungodly decisions, which contradict the wisdom we are given in God's Word. To live out godly wisdom, you first must have a relationship with Jesus Christ. Having turned from your sins and placed your faith and trust in Him alone for your salvation, you will be able to walk wisely.

Sarah's story, however, doesn't end in shame and despair. She made a decision during her sophomore year to receive the grace and forgiveness of Jesus Christ, surrendering her life (and the baggage that included) over to Him, and laying it all at the foot of the cross. She then followed through in believer's baptism a few weeks after that decision. That night in Sarah's life was the beginning of a new chapter for her! She is now growing in her faith and trying to make wise decisions in her life as she pursues a daily walk with Jesus Christ.

So a major key for you to grasp in order to live victoriously and avoid the pitfalls of the college experience begins and ends with Jesus. It is Jesus alone who will forever truly fulfill and satisfy our deepest desires and longings. He is the only true fulfillment to this longing within us. All too often, we chase so many other things from our world and our culture in order to attempt to fulfill and validate us. We lack wisdom in what we pursue. However, it's pretty much a guarantee that these pitfalls leave many hurt, broken, and empty with baggage that they will carry around for the rest of their lives. A lack of wisdom in your daily choices can result in consequences that will leave you with scars. But it doesn't have to.

Remember, it is wisdom that will keep you from falling into the typical college experience, and your college experience will be determined by the wisdom you possess. Lack of wisdom will lead to reckless behavior, while spiritual wisdom will lead to righteous living.

Andy Stanley wrote a book called *The Best Question Ever*, in which he says that the best question ever is not what is the right thing to do, but what is the wise thing to do. This is a book that I highly recommend for students to read in high school and beyond when it comes to desiring wisdom for your life. Take, for example, the difference between wisdom and knowledge as you would approach a crosswalk on a college campus. Every student at the University of Arkansas *knows* that each crosswalk on campus requires a driver to stop for any and every pedestrian. Wisdom, however, would say you still better use caution and look both ways before you step off of that curb, or you might get hit by the student who is driving distracted on their cell phone.

In order to make wise decisions, we must step back and evaluate a given situation and ask ourselves whether a certain choice will bring good and blessing to our lives or bring heartache and destruction. Many of us walk through life asking the wrong questions—we shouldn't just be asking what is right or wrong, but instead ask what is the *wise thing* to do. When we learn to redirect our questions, it will greatly impact our decision-making process.

The nineteenth-century English pastor Charles Spurgeon put it this way:

> Wisdom is the right use of knowledge. To know is not to be wise. Many men know a great deal, and are all the greater fools for it. There is no fool so great a fool as a knowing fool. But to know how to use knowledge is to have wisdom.[1]

*To apply wisdom, we must know what is wise, and there is no better place to look to for wisdom than in the Word of God, specifically in the book of Proverbs. The book of Proverbs is full of verses that speak to what wisdom is and what wisdom is not.* "Blessed are those who find wisdom, those who gain understanding" (Prov. 3:13 NIV). King Solomon said in Proverbs 24:13–14 (ESV), "My son, eat honey, for it is good, and the drippings of the honeycomb are sweet to your taste. Know that wisdom is such to your soul; if you find it, there will be a future, and your hope will not be cut off." Wisdom herself speaks in Proverbs 8:32–36:

> And now, sons, listen to me; those who keep my ways are happy. Listen to instruction and be wise; don't ignore it. Anyone who listens to me is happy, watching at my doors every day, waiting by the posts of my doorway. For the one who finds me finds life and obtains favor from the LORD, but the one who misses me harms himself; all who hate me love death.

Wisdom leads to a hope-filled life. Committing verses like these found in the book of Proverbs to memory will leave you better equipped to face aspects of college head-on with a mature and wise mind-set as you recall the Word of God that you have

---

[1] https://www.quotes.net/quote/44272

committed to memory. You must capitalize on wisdom in order to avoid the pitfalls of the college experience.

## Applying Wisdom

Recognizing what wisdom is and where it comes from is the first step, but how do we *apply* the wisdom needed to live a godly life? Wisdom will be displayed in how you carry yourself through life and how you handle new situations and experiences as they arise. A wise person who strives to live out their college years in a way that honors the Lord will discipline himself or herself to recall the Scriptures that he or she has put to memory, and to ask the right question: *What is the wise thing to do?*

As you apply godly wisdom, it will help you to avoid these pitfalls in this new season of your life. That's why it's imperative for you to be in God's Word daily. Don't only spend time daily in God's Word, but seek out those people in your life who you can go to for godly counsel about life and the decisions that you are being faced with throughout college. Having godly accountability in your life when it comes to applying wisdom is imperative. A different college experience will require that you live a life that is different than most, one that imitates the life of Christ, as in Ephesians 5:1: "Therefore, be imitators of God, as dearly loved children." We don't choose to live our lives differently in order to be saved; we live differently because we are saved. There is a strong application here for us as Christ followers: as we live the life that Christ has for us, it has got to be a lifestyle of godliness more than just a label that we claim to possess.

My story with God starts out like the majority of others who call the Bible Belt home. I've heard all God has to say in His Word since day one. I heard the gospel and experienced salvation by grace through faith in Jesus alone at a young age. When I became a teenager, though, I started listening to something different. Peer pressure. Lust. Pride. I remember thinking to myself, *I'm young, so I can live how I want to live now and come back to this Jesus lifestyle later.* What a bad thought that led to even worse choices of pornography, pride in my athletics, and other sinful postures.

That's when God taught me to be wise the hard way. When I was fifteen and not walking with Jesus, our church got a new youth pastor, Randy Presley. Honestly, I didn't like the guy at first, but God used him in an incredible way to bring me back to God. He left the ninety-nine sheep to go after the one—me. Randy and I started getting closer as the year went on. He started teaching me all that it meant to live my life with faith in Jesus. I came to a moment after my first mission trip to Zambia where the Lord took me to my knees in prayer. In that moment I realized I could keep living stubbornly trying to find satisfaction and fun in places that left me empty, or I could repent from all that to what God had to offer. The next few years of high school I had left I spent with great godly friends and trying to reach my football team with this gospel that filled my life. Then, it was off to Fayetteville.

It wasn't too far into my college moments that my friends talked me into going to a house party—even before the first day of class. As soon as we walked in the door, it was as if I had walked onto the set of any college-based movie filled with beer pong, hooking up, and red Solo cups. I remember it only took me forty-five minutes to decide not only to leave the party, but that life had nothing valuable to offer me.

The good news is that walking with Jesus doesn't really come along with a case of FOMO (fear of missing out). It's not as if there are only two options—choice A, the party, or B, sitting in your dorm and just going to class. There is a choice C, and it's Christ, along with all the joy and good times He has to offer inside godly community.

A month after that party, I met great friends like Taylor Lindley, who is still my best friend to this day. I actually had friends who cared about me as a person instead of pressuring me to become what they wanted me to be. My college experience was filled with road trips, camping trips, and house parties without alcohol, so I could actually remember the fun I had. I actually got to see how serving the church was life-giving and fun, not just a task. Small group Bible study became friends and me caring, challenging, and enjoying each other in life. My study abroad experience in Spain wasn't wasted getting wasted. It opened my eyes up to a whole new people and culture God loves while getting to surf pristine beaches, hike beautiful landscapes, try crazy-good food, learn Salsa dancing, and enjoy people from all over.

I had learned my lesson as a teenager. I'd rather listen to godly wisdom than have to be brought to repentance. I'm thankful God is a great, gracious Father who accepts me back after repenting and teaches me wisdom from my mistakes. But I'm much more thankful and much less scarred when I humbly follow Jesus, maybe not knowing everything but still reaping the joy of living faithfully with Him. Because I walked away from the party scene and walked in the wisdom God had given to me, I didn't miss out on anything in college. So choose the wisdom given by God rather than wisdom earned through mistakes.

—Zach Morris

James 1:5 says, "Now if any of you lacks wisdom, he should ask God—who gives to all generously and ungrudgingly—and it will be given to him." All you have to do is ask God for wisdom. Just ask Him for it! If we will be open and lean into His goodness, He is a good and loving Father who wants to give wisdom to us generously. King Solomon, in 1 Kings 3:9, could have asked God for numerous things, but the one thing he asked of the Lord was for wisdom. He would later go on to write much of the book of Proverbs and many of the verses from that book that we read earlier. Like King Solomon, all we need to do is ask God for His wisdom, and then be courageous enough to apply that wisdom to our lives by living a life that is different!

# Chapter 9

# Gaining Wisdom

**TO GAIN SPIRITUAL WISDOM** means you must begin by making Jesus your Lord. In the life of a believer, in order for you to gain spiritual wisdom it will require spiritual development and growth. When the lordship of Jesus is a settled issue in one's life, it settles all other issues. When we define Jesus as our Lord, we are simply submitting ourselves under His authority over our lives. By definition, the word *Lord* is defined as "someone or something having power, authority, or influence; a master or ruler." When we submit to His love, authority, and position in our life, it should change our view of Him in light of who we are and how small we are in the grand scheme of creation. "If we live, we live for the Lord; and if we die, we die for the Lord. So, whether we live or die, we belong to the Lord. Christ died and returned to life for this: that he might be Lord over both the dead and the living" (Rom. 14:8–9).

There is probably an adult in your life that you hold a "healthy fear" of. Whether it's a parent, a coach, a teacher, or a boss, you have a healthy fear of them because in light of who you are as a student or young adult, they have authority over you. The same is true of our view of God. When we view ourselves in light of who He is, how much He knows, what all He has planned for our life—that changes everything! Wisdom comes as we grow to develop a healthy fear of the Lord as we discussed in the previous chapter. When we make Jesus our Lord, a life of wisdom will follow because we then have the power, presence, and conviction of the Holy Spirit present and active in our lives to help us withstand the pitfalls that will lie before us.

The Lord never called us to be perfect, but the presence of the Holy Spirit in our lives brings peace, conviction, guidance, wisdom, and truth. In 1 Corinthians 6:19–20 we are reminded that we are a temple of the Holy Spirit: "Don't you know that your body is a temple of the Holy Spirit who is in you, whom you have from God? You are not your own, for you were bought at a price. So glorify God with your body."

Receiving the Holy Spirit into our life following salvation provides us with a supernatural strength to overcome the pitfalls and temptations of our flesh. Jesus teaches us this in Matthew 26:41, "Watch and pray so that you will not fall into temptation. The spirit is willing, but the flesh is weak" (NIV). Apart from the activity of the Spirit in our lives, we cannot live out and apply spiritual wisdom. One of the most practical gifts the Holy Spirit brings into your life following salvation is conviction. When you feel a sense of heaviness or discomfort within you when you're faced with a situation that requires spiritual wisdom, you need to listen to that "still, small voice." It's like a flashing caution sign in your life, blinking and shining brightly, warning you of the danger ahead! Take heed to that warning. Listen to that voice. And as you grow in your walk with the Lord, spending time in His Word, and in prayer, this supernatural power is awakened within you.

When you take into consideration all that has been done for you, remembering the cross where Jesus took your place, and living a changed life than before with great gratitude for the gift of the Holy Spirit in your life, that is what changes you! It is the power of God in and through us that gives us the source of strength we need to live out spiritual wisdom and avoid the traps and pitfalls that the enemy will throw in our way.

## TO GAIN WISDOM, YOU MUST . . .

### Desire Wisdom

You pursue what you desire and you will never gain something that you don't desire. When a man desires a woman, he pursues her . . . and just a side note for a whole other chapter—it is the man's job to be the one to pursue, not the other way around. When I, Brian Mills, knew I wanted to date my now-wife, Jennifer, I had to work hard and pursue after her. She and I had ended up at odds with each other due to some unfortunate circumstances in our friendship and she was not into me at all. Yet, the Lord had changed my heart and I knew she was the girl that the Lord had for me. So what did I do? I pursued. When you desire someone, you pursue them. I pursued her with everything I had.

If you long to live a life of wisdom and avoid the pitfalls of the college experience, you must *pursue* wisdom. "Prize her highly, and she will exalt you; she will honor you if you embrace her" (Prov. 4:8 ESV). We will never gain what we don't desire. In my time of ministry and in meeting with college students, I have had many say to me, "Pastor Brian, I just wanted to have these four years to myself and to live it up while here in college, but I will straighten back up post-college, once this season of my life is over and I'm ready to settle down." What they are saying is, "I desire worldliness over godliness," and as a result they load up on baggage and scars from their college experience. Unwise living ALWAYS will lead to a life full of baggage that you will carry with you throughout the rest of your life. Wisdom in this would tell you that the decisions you make today will affect your life tomorrow.

You will not gain something that you do not desire. Pursue a life of godly wisdom and live a life that will leave an impact and a legacy in others' lives, not just leave a blip of a memory of you behind when you graduate. You will either be remembered for the great and impactful things you have done with this gift of a life you've been given, or you will be remembered for failures or mistakes, but the choice is yours and what you pursue. This pertains to each and every season of your life, including the college years. But you must desire it and be proactive to set goals in your life, particularly in your spiritual life. We only have one shot at this life we've been given. There is no dress rehearsal, scrimmage, or practice round. Think proactively and look ahead and dream big about how are you going to live this one life that you've been given to make the biggest impact for the gospel of Jesus Christ and the purposes that He has for you here on this earth.

The author of the book of Hebrews gives us a great snapshot of a runner and the finish line when it refers to our life in Hebrews 12:1–2. If we view this life as a race, each one of us has been entrusted with OUR race. It's not the person to our right or left, our family, our coach, or our pastors—it's our race and it's our job to run our race well with everything that we have. However, we can't get lost in comparison looking at those to our right or left, nor can we have a do-over. But the good news is that we don't have to run this race alone, we're equipped with everything we will ever need because of Christ in our life. Jesus knew that we couldn't do this thing called life on our own or in our own strength. That's why He is right there with us and challenges us to fix our eyes on Him, "the source and perfecter of our faith." Even with all the power of positive thinking and our own best intentions, we can't do it. But He did. He endured and won this overall race by conquering death on the cross once and for all so He could return to heaven where He is seated at the right hand of God the Father cheering us on from the "grandstand" fan section, watching us run our race yet beckoning us to FIX our eyes on Him and Him alone to reach the finish line, and hear Him say at the end, like He did in Matthew 25:23, "Well done, good and faithful servant!"

### Know the Word of God

You become like the people you hang out with, so if you want to become like Christ you must spend time WITH CHRIST, in His Word. How can you have a relationship with someone that you do not know? "Imitate God, therefore, in everything you do, because you are his dear children" (Eph. 5:1 NLT).

One of my favorite things to do is spend time with my family. I love taking my wife on dates, being at all my children's extra-curricular activities, and just spending time hanging out together with them. As a result of the time I spend with my wife and with my kids, I know my family really well. I know how to bring joy to their lives and I also know what causes sadness in their lives. I know my family really well, not only because they are my family but because I spend time with them. What good would it be if I saw my family once a year and never spoke to them? We would still be a family unit but we definitely would not be a close family.

Yet this is what we do as believers. We give our life to Christ and are grateful we are "saved," yet we spend no time getting to know Christ on a day-to-day basis and developing our relationship with Him. Most don't live out the wisdom of the Word because they don't know the wisdom of the Word. You have to be in the Word of God to know the Word of God, which is how we get to know Him personally. This is the key to where wisdom is found. A spiritual discipline that I do in my own personal time with the Lord is that I read the *One Year Chronological Bible* every year. It's easy to understand as it threads all of Scripture together with such an awesome redemptive thread, and reading it in chronological order makes it easier to understand by grouping together all the events of Scripture with when it occurred. So when you read about King Hezekiah's life in 2 Kings 18, it will also include in that day's reading where it speaks of King Hezekiah's life in 2 Chronicles 29. It combines in each day's reading each section of Scripture that is included in that time line, grouping it all together with the time line of Scripture and of history.

It's vital for the life of a believer to be in God's Word, reading and meditating on it daily. Reading the Word of God leads to obedience in the life of a believer; however, you cannot be obedient to what you do not know. When you are in the Word of God, reading it, memorizing Scripture, you begin to see the wisdom that is ours to possess that is only possible through our time with the Lord. "For the LORD gives wisdom; from his mouth come knowledge and understanding" (Prov. 2:6 NIV). How can you get wisdom from the Lord if you do not spend time with the Lord? If you are going to avoid the pitfalls of the college experience you *must* spend time in the Word *daily*. Let me interject here that reading and spending time in the Word daily is not enough. *Reflect daily on the time you spent in the Word; don't just spend time in the Word without allowing it to change you.*

We learn from reflecting back on our experiences, not simply by our experiences alone. Reflecting means intentionally looking back with purpose. When we pause and reflect, it often causes us to bear witness to all the ways the Lord is speaking to us, or is there, showing up, equipping, providing, or intervening, and we could absolutely miss His faithfulness if we don't take time to pause and reflect on what we read in our time with Him in His Word. Whether it's journaling or keeping a note of simple bullet points of what the Lord has taught you and what He has done in your life, you can go back and remember all that He has done so it can strengthen your faith moving forward that He is faithful and good.

If we read and never reflect or evaluate, how can we apply what we have read to our lives? In doing this, we stunt the growth and sanctification process in our spiritual life. It's like an athlete who goes back after a game to watch game film from the previous game. Why do they do that? To get better. They're looking back to study and evaluate so they can be a better player and athlete. Same for us in our spiritual walk; we should pause and take time to reflect and remember.

### Have an Effective Prayer Life

"But seek first his kingdom and his righteousness, and all these things will be given to you as well" (Matt. 6:33 NIV).

I truly believe we have not, because we ask not. As Jesus was teaching His disciples in John 16:23–24, ". . . anything you ask the Father in my name, he will give you. Until now you have asked for nothing in my name. Ask and you will receive, so that your joy may be complete." Going to the Lord daily in prayer is the single greatest thing you can do as a believer. We are called to seek His face, and He promises all throughout Scripture that IF we seek Him, we will FIND Him, IF we seek Him with ALL of our hearts. Wisdom leads us to pray, to seek Him out, and to seek His will for our lives. We realize we NEED Him, and we can't do this life alone without Him, His presence, His power, His wisdom, and His strength in this life.

Solomon asked for one thing from the Lord in 1 Kings 3:8–12:

> "Your servant is among your people you have chosen, a people too many to be numbered or counted. So give your servant a receptive heart to judge your people and to discern between good and evil. For who is able to judge this great people of yours?"
>
> Now it pleased the Lord that Solomon had requested this. So God said to him, "Because you have requested this and did not ask for long life or riches for yourself, or the death of your enemies, but you asked discernment for yourself to administer justice, I will therefore do what you have asked. I will give you a wise and understanding

heart, so that there has never been anyone like
you before and never will be again."

When you spend time with the Lord, you move beyond the
desires of self and selfish ambitions and you begin to pray for God's
activity in our life. We need a group of people to rise up who are
daily hitting their knees for their sphere of influence in which
they have been placed. We need the people of God to become
prayer warriors to God. Solomon gained the wisdom he desired
from his prayer life because he asked God for it. When you are
praying for wisdom to avoid your pitfalls, you are less likely to fall
into the pit.

Let me challenge you today to create some intentionality
when it comes to your prayer life. You will never have an effective
prayer life until you get intentional with your prayer time, and
being intentional in your time helps when you create a prayer
list. Know what you pray for daily and evaluate your list often, be
intentional with your time in prayer before the Lord, put Scripture
to the requests on your list and cry out to God on your knees daily
for those specific requests.

Throughout history, spiritual movements began because of
a powerful and effective prayer life of a believer. In 1857, the
North Dutch Church in New York City hired a businessman,
Jeremiah Lanphier, to be a lay missionary. He prayed, "Lord,
what would You have me do?" Concerned by the anxious faces of
businessmen on the streets of New York City, Lanphier decided
to open the church at noon so businessmen could pray. The
first meeting was set for September 23—three weeks before the
Bank Panic of 1857. Six attended the first week, twenty the next,
then forty, then they switched to daily meetings. Before long
all the space was taken, and other churches also began to open
up for businessmen's prayer meetings. Revivals broke out every-
where in 1857, spreading throughout the United States and the
world. Sometimes called The Great Prayer Meeting Revival, an

estimated one million people were added to America's church rolls, and as many as one million of the four million existing church members also converted.[1] This was known as the Businessmen's Revival of 1857–1858.

There is great power when God's people pray. If we want to see a movement happen in our generation today . . . PRAY!

I have traveled to fifteen states and one other country and have run over 22,000 miles in my ten years of being a student athlete. I have had opportunities to run at the highest national and world levels in cross country. Along with the successes, I have experienced a handful of setbacks. These experiences have not only instilled in me the importance of health, but they have taught me more about myself and my God. If I never learned how to take ownership of my own health both physically and spiritually, then I would have missed the plan God intended for me.

Taking the step from a high school student athlete to a University of Arkansas student athlete made me aware of the state of my health. Right away, I was thrown into utter mental, physical, and spiritual depravation. I could no longer continue building up my physical health and merely maintain my spiritual health. For as it says in 1 Timothy 4:8, "Physical training is of some value, but godliness has value for all things, holding promise for both the present life and the life to come" (NIV).

I had to learn how to train my spirit in the same way I was training my body. By seeking God in His Word, prayer, church, and community, I was training my spirit. Each time I submitted myself under God's presence, I was training my spirit. As with training my body, I had to practice diligence and endurance, trusting that despite the setbacks I faced, I would experience even more godliness because of them. The impact of spiritual training extends past the impact of physical training. When I neglect to train my body, I see momentary changes in

---

[1] J. Edwin Orr, *The Event of the Century* (Wheaton, IL: International Awakening Press, 1989), 52–56, 320–21.

my mood and appearance, but when I neglect to train my spirit, I see dramatic shifts in who I am. God designed this difference to highlight the level of importance. Physical training is important, but only temporarily. I adjust to a lack of training with minimal effects. But spiritual training is eternal. When I neglect to train my spirit, I lose joy, patience, peace, and love—all of which I cannot adjust to.

College is a time for genuine training that you must take ownership of. If you do not choose to train your spirit to reach godly health, then you will miss the plan that God intended for you.

The places I have traveled and the thousands of miles I have run would have been pointless if I failed to see God's plan in them. God has a plan for all of us, and it starts with training your spirit in godliness. I urge you to take just one step in training your spirit. Whether it be reading the Bible, praying more intentionally, committing to church, or joining a small group, one step is all it takes for God to begin to strengthen your spirit.

—Kelsey Schrader, senior at University of Arkansas; cross-country runner

## Chapter 10

# Living Wisely

**TO GAIN WISDOM YOU** must evaluate who you are allowing to "breathe into you." First Corinthians 15:33 says, "Do not be deceived: 'Bad company corrupts good morals.'"

Have you ever heard the expression, "You become like the people you hang out with"? This statement is profoundly true. Who we let into our lives will affect what comes out. In Luke 6:45, Jesus says, "A good person produces good out of the good stored up in his heart. An evil person produces evil out of the evil stored up in his heart, for his mouth speaks from the overflow of the heart." What comes out of your life is determined by what you allow in. What you allow in is determined by who you surround yourself with, and this includes social media, what you watch, what you listen to, and who you spend time with.

## Wisdom in Choosing Friends

Many college students feel the only way to meet people and make friends is rushing and pledging a sorority or fraternity. This is a great means for relationship, social life, and friendship, but choose wisdom here. Ask yourself good questions before you jump into these or any other communities of friends, and pray for wisdom in choosing which organizations to be a part of.

*Who are these people?*

*What do they stand for?*

*What do they value?*

*What positive things will this group bring to my life?*

On the flip side of evaluating a decision to be a part of Greek life on a college campus, there is great opportunity to be a light in a dark place. There have been so many great ministry opportunities and lives changed by believers who lived out their faith in their sorority or fraternity house. You can definitely make your mark and be a difference-maker as well. The relationships that are formed through Greek life will be great if done with wisdom. But it's not only about who you are influencing, but who you allow to breathe into your life that matters.

This applies to all organizations you're a part of and the friends you select. It matters. Always look for those who share the same values and convictions you do. Those people are out there. You've just got to look for them, pray for them, and put yourself in environments to find them. The most fertile ground for these friends is—you guessed it—in the local church, which is just another reason we are called to be active members of a church.

Community is something we all innately desire. We all desire to belong and have a place and a people to do life with. This is a good desire placed in us by God. But we must be careful to make sure those people spur us on and point us toward Jesus. This is vital for you to live a life of wisdom, especially through your college years.

For you to understand the importance of community, you must grasp the power that others have over who you allow to breathe into you on a regular basis. In order to avoid the pitfalls of the college experience, you must grasp that the church community you join is more important for your spiritual health and well-being than the campus organization you pick.

One of the most important tools you can have at your disposal in college is community. God didn't make us to be solitary creatures, but He gave us community as a gift to help us in our sanctification. In college, who you surround yourself with will affect who you become. It is very easy to get caught up in the ways of the world when you surround yourself with people who are chasing after the things of this world. On the flip side, it is very easy to get caught up in the ways of God when you surround yourself with people who are chasing after the things of God. Proverbs 27:17 says, "Iron sharpens iron, and one person sharpens another." This is God's design. The one sure-fire place to find this community that will sharpen you and help you grow closer to God is in the church.

I underestimated how hard the transition to college life would be. I've always hated change, and going to college is everything changing at once. I went from a place where I knew everyone to a place where I hardly knew anyone. All of my safety nets were gone, and I had never truly learned to rely on the Lord. I retreated. My freshman year of college, I hardly made any new friends. I still had my friends from home, but I didn't make much of an attempt to find a new community. I didn't get plugged into any organizations, campus ministries, or a local church. The only time I went to church my freshman year was when I was home. This was easily the farthest away I had ever been from God, yet He blessed me by keeping me away from the party scene, depression, or any of the other things I could have fallen into. It is easy for me to see now how much God was still pursuing me when I wasn't pursuing Him at all.

I found myself praying that God would give me a community of fellow believers to help push me and hold me accountable in my faith. I found that my sophomore year at Cross Church. I've been involved in a couple of campus ministries, and those are great, but nowhere have I found a community like I have at church. Acts 2:46–47 paints the perfect picture of what the church should be when it says, "Every day they devoted themselves to meeting together in the temple, and broke bread from house to house. They ate their food with joyful and sincere hearts, praising God and enjoying the favor of all the people. Every day the Lord added to their number those who were being saved." This is what the church does. It provides us with a group of people to do life with, the good and the bad. This is a gift straight from God which I praise Him for every day, and one that every college student should seek out diligently.

—Devin Dupree, University of Arkansas; junior medical student

## Identity and Wisdom

"So God created mankind in his own image, in the image of God he created them; male and female he created them" (Gen. 1:27 niv).

Where we locate our identity is going to be where we find our hope and purpose. The American dream tells us our hope is found in success, money, appearance, how many likes we get on social media, and so much more. So often, even as believers, we find our identity and value in the things society tells us we should find it in, rather than who Christ made us to be. When you look in the mirror, do you say, "God loves me, God designed me, God gifted me, God forgave me, God created me, and God gives me grace"? You might know, intellectually, that God loves you, but does it seep down into your heart? You might know God designed you, but are you happy with His design of you, the one He created in His image? You might know God gifted you, but are you using your gifts to bring Him glory?

You see, so many times, we know what God has done, but we often find it hard to believe it or receive it for ourselves and it let it affect how we define ourselves. Who you portray yourself to be is who people will believe you are. And God says you are His—chosen in Christ, an adopted child, forgiven, loved, valued.

It's crucial for us to find our identity in Christ and Christ alone! He is our creator, our savior, our cheerleader, and our biggest fan . . . He's our student section. "You did not choose me," He said to His disciples, "but I chose you. I appointed you to go and produce fruit and that your fruit should remain, so that whatever you ask the Father in my name, he will give you" (John 15:16).

The Bible also tells us about how much God values us and how intentionally He created us in Psalm 139:13–16:

> For it was you who created my inward parts; you knit me together in my mother's womb. I will praise you because I have been remarkably and wondrously made. Your works are wondrous, and I know this very well. My bones were not hidden from you when I was made in secret, when I was formed in the depths of the earth. Your eyes saw me when I was formless; all my days were written in your book and planned before a single one of them began.

Don't miss this. You were knit together in your mother's womb by the very hand of God Almighty. God knows your body and is pleased with His creation—your value and validation does not come from how many likes your images get on Instagram or how many reps you can get in the gym with the guys. I often say, "You will attract what you dress to attract." Do you find your identity more in your abs or your figure than you do in Christ and in who He says that you are?

Another thing that can skew our identity is our past. It's so important for you to understand this: your past *does not* define your future. You are not your past. For every believer, we must believe and claim the freedom from our past—that Jesus has forgiven and cleansed us from every sin and has thrown it "as far as the east is from the west," according to Psalm 103:12. So why do we keep going back to it and picking up the baggage of our forgiven past and choosing to carry it around with us in our new life in Christ? Scripture says in John 10:10 that we have a real enemy, a thief who comes to "steal and kill and destroy," but Jesus says, "I have come so that they may have life and have it in abundance." The enemy wants you to be so distracted by the noise from our culture or from your past so you won't be able to hear the truth from the Word of God about who He is and who He says that you are.

All of us have believed lies about ourselves. It's time to lay them down. It's time to quit believing the lie from Satan that there is no hope for you or you can't break free from who you were, or what you experienced in your past. You may say that you know you're forgiven but you don't feel forgiven because of the baggage you brought into your relationship with Christ, but if you're in Christ, you're a new creation—the old has gone, the new has come (2 Cor. 5:17). And just as 1 John 1:9 says, "If we confess our sins, he is faithful and righteous to forgive us our sins and to cleanse us from all unrighteousness."

Live in this promise of freedom for your future when it comes to your identity in Christ. You must know who He says that you are in order to believe it and you will only find that in the Word of God.

## Wise Boundaries

"As obedient children, do not be conformed to the desires of your former ignorance. But as the one who called you is holy, you also are to be holy in all your conduct; for it is written, 'Be holy, because I am holy'" (1 Pet. 1:14–16).

The college experience is one of nearly unlimited freedom and experiences, which can lead to great temptation if you're not prepared for it. When you don't have clear and firm boundaries, you can't experience true freedom. It seems counterintuitive, but wisdom screams to set boundaries that lead toward a life of wise decision-making.

It's like driving a boat. I grew up on a lake in Hot Springs, Arkansas. When I was a kid, I would take the boat out. There were obvious boundaries about where I could go and what I could do. I could drive it as fast as I wanted on either side of the lake and make sudden turns if I desired.

There's a lot of freedom in driving a boat, but there was always one place I couldn't go . . . land! If I desired to drive it on land, only destruction would happen. Why? Because I would be leaving the boundaries for which it was created. A boat is meant to be driven in the water; likewise, God has given us clear boundaries for our lives in His Word. If we follow His Word and set our boundaries based on the guidelines and parameters from His Word, we will experience complete and true freedom. They are there for our protection and guidance, not to oppress us. Galatians 5:13 says, "For you were called to be free, brothers and sisters; only don't use this freedom as an opportunity for the flesh, but serve one another through love." We are called to live free, but not called to live without godly boundaries.

As believers, we are called to be holy by not being conformed to the world. This simply means we are set apart. We cannot be passive about our sin and still be holy. We must recognize our weakness, know how the enemy targets us, and be proactive by setting boundaries for our lives.

First Peter 5:8 says, "Be sober-minded, be alert. Your adversary the devil is prowling around like a roaring lion, looking for anyone he can devour." Set boundaries that lead to holiness—living set apart. Holiness demands living a life of wisdom. I have yet to see a Christian who can withstand the temptation of sin without setting boundaries in place to keep them from falling into the temptation to sin. We will talk about this more in-depth later.

Holiness is a requirement for us to avoid the pitfalls of the college experience. A life of holiness is a life lived with wise boundaries in place.

# Part 5

# Relationships

# Chapter 11

# Guardrails

**THE DIVORCE RATE IS** ever growing. Affairs seem to be considered almost acceptable, as long as people are being authentic to their "true love." Access to pornography is at an all-time high, and relationships seem to be struggling today more than ever before. This is what I like to call, "the acceptable norm," and it is taking us away from God's design for us when it comes to our relationships.

Obviously, there is a huge disparity between our cultural view of dating and relationships and the Bible's view. Our hope over these next few chapters is to move you toward godly wisdom when it comes to your relationships.

Our culture today seems to expect you to "test drive" your relationships through the standards of the world versus committing to a relationship that will bring glory to God. This often happens through cohabitation, sex before marriage, pornography, one-night stands, and lust. No one goes into a relationship with the intentions to hurt or destroy the other person involved, but it seems to be the normal result of the way we handle relationships in our culture today.

## Guardrails

We want to help you succeed in your relationships and honor one another. We are confident this is possible, but we do have to take a different approach than our world takes. A key to having healthy relationships is having healthy boundaries. Just like guardrails keep us safe while driving around a curve or on a winding highway, all relationships need guardrails in place that can keep you from "falling off the cliff" in your relationships.

A relationship without guardrails is a relationship without convictions. John 16:8 says about the Holy Spirit, "When he comes, he will convict the world about sin, righteousness, and judgment." This simply means that the Holy Spirit will convict us of wrong. The first work of the Holy Spirit in the life of a believer is the conviction of his or her sin. If we are to be temples of the Holy Spirit, where His presence dwells, He will convict us of our sin.

If you are a follower of Christ, you will face the conviction of the Holy Spirit. If you evaluate your life and can say you never feel convicted, I would seriously evaluate whether or not you truly have surrendered your life under the authority and lordship of Jesus Christ. If you have, Scripture tells us that we possess His Holy Spirit in our lives as a helper and teacher to guide and direct our lives. Jesus explains this to His disciples in John 14:16–17, "And I will ask the Father, and he will give you another Helper, to be with you forever, even the Spirit of truth, whom the world cannot receive, because it neither sees him or knows him. You know him, for he dwells with you and will be in you" (ESV).

So let me ask you today, when it comes to your relationships, have you ever thought about any personal convictions about guardrails that you desire to implement in your life and relationships?

Let me see if I can give you a few.

### Spend Time with God Daily

We said in the last chapter that you become like the people you spend time with. If you want to act like Christ, you must spend time with Him. I know this is a chapter on relationships, but you will never act like Christ desires for you to in your relationships if spending time with Christ is not part of your daily routine.

I would encourage you to do this in the morning. A runner will never get ready for a race after the race is over. Those who prepare have a higher chance to succeed than those who do not. Why would we treat our day-to-day spiritual walk any differently? Prepare for your day by spending time with God before your day begins. Mark 1:35 says, "Very early in the morning, while it was still dark, [Jesus] got up, went out, and made his way to a deserted place; and there he was praying." Let me challenge you to do the same.

### "Not Even a Hint"

The second guardrail I would encourage you to implement in your relationships is "not even a hint" (Eph. 5:3 NIV). "But among you," the apostle Paul says, "there must not be even a hint of sexual immorality, or of any kind of impurity, or of greed, because these are improper for God's holy people." Let's admit up front that this is a huge challenge. Due to the tragic pornography epidemic in our culture today, the dress code that screams, "lust after me," and the craftiness of the enemy, most of our relationships are a lust-filled disaster. Couples in college are cohabiting more than ever before, "hooking up" has become a flippant and normal part of modern-day life and relationships, we spend hours in front of the mirror being sure the various parts of our body are featured just right, and as a result, it is much more than just a hint. In fact, it has become more blatant than subtle, and all in the attempt to lure the affection and attention of the opposite sex.

What would happen if we followed Ephesians 5:3 with great conviction? Does that mean everyone should wear baggy pants and turtleneck sweaters even in the dead heat of August? No!

But it will take more vigilance, which will result in greater health when it comes to our relationships.

Relationships that are more focused on the physical than the spiritual and emotional are relationships that are destined to fail. If you can have a powerful sexual moment with someone but can't carry on a decent conversation, then you may be in lust, but you are not in love. Many today are falling for lustful moments of passion over true love, because they have never set the guardrail of "not even a hint."

I want to be clear here, this is not just an attempt to give you another list of "do's and don'ts," nor set you up for a legalistic lifestyle when it comes to your relationships. I do, however, want to inspire you to pursue a life of holiness—one that is centered on honoring the Word of God. Here is how you can do so practically.

It all begins with recognizing your weaknesses. You can't change what you don't know needs to change. To follow the guardrail of "not even a hint" from Ephesians 5:3, you must recognize what your "hints" are. Some weaknesses we all share. We are all driven and tempted sexually—in one way or another. The one who believes he or she is above falling into the trap of lust is the one who inevitably falls. The question is, are you convicted when you are tempted, and if so, what do you do about it? A repentant heart should be shared within the relationship, not just displayed on one side.

Second, take the action step to memorize Scripture that attacks your weaknesses. Nothing attacks sin like Scripture. Post it around your dorm room, your apartment, in your car, on your bathroom mirror, wherever you will see it. Bathe your life and your mind with the Word of God. The Word of God is our only offensive weapon in the spiritual battles we face in life. The rest of the armor of God listed in Ephesians 6 is armor for our protection, it's defensive. If you're going to fight off your enemy, who is very real, very intentional, and is coming after you with no other objective than to steal, kill, and destroy you, according to John 10:10, then you must fight offensively with God's Word.

Read it. Know it. Memorize it.

Lastly, run from all temptation. Scripture speaks clearly to this in 2 Timothy 2:22, "Run from temptations that capture young people. Always do the right thing" (cev). Since we know we are all susceptible and we can all fall into temptation, we must be prepared to run when it comes—and it will come. Are you willing to walk out of the party because the temptation is too strong? Are you willing to unfollow that individual because the pictures posted by them are causing you to stumble? None of the above mean you are some kind of pervert; it simply means you're human, you're recognizing your temptation, and taking proactive measures to put guardrails in place in your life to avoid falling. It means that you are striving for purity and for godliness.

### Date Someone Who Loves Jesus

The third guardrail is, if you date someone, date someone who loves Jesus. Second Corinthians 6:15 says, "What does a believer have in common with an unbeliever?" There is something unique about allowing your heart to be vulnerable through a relationship. College is a time where you will explore the experience and processes of "doing life" alongside someone, which eventually can lead into a marriage covenant. Through this exploration, you will recognize that your life is strongly influenced and highly impacted by this one person. Your actions, decisions, language, emotions, wants, and desires begin to echo and mirror theirs. That is why it is a game changer—because who you date falls in line with the convictions of your heart. You have to ask, why would you choose to date someone today that you would not choose to marry in the future, and why would you choose to date someone not currently going on the same life path you are on?

As a follower of Christ, you should be on a daily pursuit of Christ and chasing after Him *independently* of another person. While pursuing Christ, if you look and see God has allowed you to meet someone of the opposite sex and they are pursuing Him on their own, then you might have found one that you should pursue to date. If you meet someone who isn't following Jesus, but you are interested in dating them, do not fall for the lie that you can change them. Let God change them before you even consider dating them. We are not the judges of another person's spiritual life, but through the fruit of a person's life, you can see where they are spiritually. Are they pursuing Christ? Do they love Christ? Are they connected to a local church? Are they being discipled and discipling others? Does their life display the spiritual fruit of health and growth from a dynamic and vibrant walk with Jesus? It's imperative that you evaluate a prospective date from this vantage point.

Date someone whose life produces godly fruit. The greatest relationships are those that challenge you. What better way to be challenged than to live out the convictions of God's Word? The one you date should spur you on, should challenge you to fully lean into all that the Lord has for your life, instead of leaning solely into them or into any other temptation that this world might lure in front of you. Our culture today is driving and speaking into the relationships of believers more than the Word of God is driving them. Don't let culture tell you who to date; allow the conviction of the Holy Spirit to keep you grounded and accountable to the Word of God.

### Garbage In, Garbage Out

This is as simple as it gets. This is a phrase that has been around computer science for many years. The phrase all started when some would pose the question, "If we put bad information into a computer, would we get the right answers?" GIGO (or Garbage In,

Garbage Out) is a computer science acronym that implies bad input will always result in bad output.[1]

According to Luke 6, GIGO is also a spiritual acronym that will play out in our lives. Jesus says:

> "A good tree doesn't produce bad fruit; on the other hand, a bad tree doesn't produce good fruit. For each tree is known by its own fruit. Figs aren't gathered from thornbushes, or grapes picked from a bramble bush. A good person produces good out of the good stored up in his heart. An evil person produces evil out of the evil stored up in his heart, for his mouth speaks from the overflow of the heart." (vv. 43–45)

The fruit of the tree defines the health of the tree. The life of a believer and follower of Jesus Christ will show the inside health of that individual. What you put in matters. We are allowing too many voices and influences into our lives today. We allow as much garbage in as we do anything.

Pornography is wrecking relationships, hookups and one-night stands leave such brokenness and baggage, abortions end unwanted pregnancies, bad advice causes constant broken hearts, FOMO (Fear of Missing Out) is leaving people empty simply because of the fear of being left out, or God forbid, being all alone on a Saturday night. We are allowing the lies our culture speaks into our relationships instead of allowing the Word of God to infiltrate our hearts and minds. Culture should not drive your relationships; the Word of God must be the driving force in your life, which in turn will drive your relationships.

Philippians 4:8 says, "Finally, brothers and sisters, whatever is true, whatever is noble, whatever is right, whatever is pure,

---

[1] https://techterms.com/definition/gigo

whatever is lovely, whatever is admirable—if anything is excellent or praiseworthy—think about such things" (NIV). Do our lives and our relationships focus on these kinds of things? Many people in your college career will try to guide you in relationships, but if their advice and "wisdom" does not line up with Philippians 4:8, tune them out, don't allow people to breathe into you who aren't pouring in godly wisdom from the Word of God.

### Go Slow

Song of Solomon 8:4 says, "Young women of Jerusalem, I charge you, do not stir up or awaken love until the appropriate time." It is easy to strike the spark of love and sexual passion before we are ready. God warns us in this verse to be patient. But we live in a culture that often ignores that wisdom and follows its own desires. Culture today pressures this idea of love and passion in various ways through movies, romance literature, images on social media, or what is expected of you from your peers. We have mistaken love for lust and the result is today's marriages are full of baggage from the past that never was dealt with and then rolls into a covenant relationship of marriage.

Let me pause here and say if you have sinned sexually in serious ways in the past, you are not defined by that sin. Our God is a redemptive God, and if you have repented and trusted in Christ, He has already forgiven you. Romans 8:1 says, "Therefore, there is now no condemnation for those in Christ Jesus." No condemnation. Remember what we said about identity earlier.

Think about this . . . "But God proves his own love for us in that *while* we were still sinners, Christ died for us" (Rom. 5:8, emphasis mine). While we were still sinners, Christ died for us. He did not wait on us to get it together or clean ourselves up first—no. He came to us, in our sin, and in the midst of our mess. First John 1:9 says, "If we confess our sins, he is faithful and righteous to forgive us our sins and to cleanse us from all unrighteousness."

Not only did He die for our sin; He forgave us of our sin. Scripture says He takes our sin upon Himself to pay the penalty we could not pay, and He separates our sin from us "as far as the east is from the west" (Ps. 103:12). This is the beauty of the redemptive story of God's amazing grace. Christ takes us back to who we were originally created to be in Genesis 1. Through His righteousness and His grace, we are forgiven. Through God's grace *you* are forgiven. Never, ever forget this powerful truth in your life!

If you've never confessed and repented of sexual sin in the past, maybe through reading this section, you can hit your knees right now in repentance and turn back to Christ and He will wash you, cleanse you, and restore you so from this day on you may chose a life of purity and abstinence, where He is in charge instead of your fleshly desires. We long for lustful, impulsive sex over sexual intimacy in marriage, which is God's design, in our relationships today. What would happen to marriages if we followed God's way over our way? What if we said we will not stir up or awaken love until the appropriate time?

Sex is a gift given by God Almighty for marriage, not a gift given by God for us to use and misuse whenever and however we please. We should enjoy this beautiful gift through marriage as God designed it to be. When you give up this gift before marriage, you are giving up what God intended for good. Remember GIGO. Sex is a form of pleasure created for a husband and wife to enjoy together as part of the intimacy of the oneness of their marriage for a lifetime, but our world has made it a part of lustful passion for us to impulsively enjoy in a moment. I have seen many relationships fail simply because all they knew how to do was to fulfill each other's lust, instead of lovingly fulfilling one another in a holistic way. Living together before marriage, or even staying in the same room together pre-marriage, always leads to greater temptation of sexual intimacy together. Be wise and go slow!

Let me share with you some boundaries from some college students about how they are going slow:

We met during a time in our lives that neither of us would say we were looking for a spouse, or even looking to date. It was completely God's timing. For the first month of knowing each other, we were in two different states and communicated through texting and phone calls. That first month was vital to our relationship, because we began to peel back layers and really get to know each other. This created a foundation of friendship for our future relationship. Once we started dating, our friendship and communication continued growing and we began to develop trust.

Our relationship was, and still is, a sanctification process. Neither of us had been in a godly relationship before, but we both knew that's what we wanted. In the beginning, honestly, it wasn't perfect. We were figuring out how we could honor God through a dating relationship, and along the way had to make changes in our personal habits and habits as a couple. Our intentions were pure, and God showed us so much grace while gently gifting us with wisdom, conviction, and courage to strengthen our relationship. Although in the beginning we felt clueless as how to have a "godly relationship," we were open with one another and willing to hand selfish desires of the flesh over to God.

Boundaries were something it felt as if we were always trying to understand. The harder we tried to discern what "good boundaries" were, the more apparent they became. The Bible makes it clear that there should not even be a hint of sexual immorality, which basically means that any form of sexuality needs to be saved for marriage. When trying to live that out for the first time, it is easy to think that God is completely against sex and wonder why He would want to keep these pleasurable things from us. Through prayer and conversation with God, it becomes evident that the Lord gives these guidelines for our protection. The scars caused by sexual sin are some of the deepest scars, and if we're being honest, most people have them. This understanding reveals that the Lord does not give us this direction with the intention of depriving us from something great, but rather to protect us and then bless us in the security of marriage.

In our dating relationship, we knew we could trust each other because there was a deep conviction in both of us anytime we crossed a boundary. We openly talked about it with one another and repented before God. We have learned that it's just as important to ask God to give you courage to change your course of action when feeling convicted as it is to pray that God will convict you. Whenever we acted out of the will of God we would feel convicted, but it was our conviction in action that was so important to the course of our relationship. After falling into sin, it is vital to have boldness to openly talk about your feelings of conviction and work with your boyfriend/girlfriend in how you can move forward from there.

One thing that was a good sign early in our relationship was that the majority of our conversations centered around the Lord. We talked about our personal God-given passions, things of this world that hurt our heart, and stories of redemption in our lives. As we began to understand each other's hearts more, we began to encourage and challenge one another to take steps of faith to advance God's kingdom. We prayed for one another and God gave us a heart to love each other more. All of this was out of the overflow of our individual love and passion for Jesus Christ.

A major key in our relationship was the community that we had surrounding us. We attended a college small group where we were welcomed and unjudged by fellow Christians. The friends that we made through that community walked with us through times of joy, times of conflict, and times of hurt. Specifically, one couple in the group poured wisdom and counsel into us while inviting us into their lives where we could observe how they glorified the Lord through their relationship. This community and these friendships were extremely important in the health of our own relationship.

By no means is our relationship perfect, but the Lord continues to grow us in Him and with each other.

—John and Ellie Wilson

## Surround Yourself with Community

Ecclesiastes 4:12 says, "And if someone overpowers one person, two can resist him. A cord of three strands is not easily broken." We often gravely underestimate the power of community in our lives. We were not created to be alone; we were created for community, particularly community with fellow believers. A relationship between a guy and girl can sometimes tend to pull each away from their same-sex friendships. A relationship in which the individuals do not have their own friendships is an unhealthy relationship. Those who solely spend time together and alone are unhealthy and will be tempted to fall into all kinds of sin.

A community of friends is a community of accountability. A relationship that does not allow you to have community is an unhealthy relationship. I would highly encourage every couple to be in a small group through their local church. While dating, it can be wise to be in an all-guys group and an all-girls group just for the sake of individual spiritual and relational growth. Those who might say, "Well, my friends/family don't like who I am dating," should heed that input and seriously evaluate your relationship for what their reasoning for that statement may be. Your friends and family could be right. God gives us community not to take us away from our significant other, but to sharpen us where we are.

## R-E-S-P-E-C-T

Philippians 2:3 says, "Do nothing out of selfish ambition or conceit, but in humility consider others as more important than yourselves." When we respect others, we lead others. Respect comes out in the way you dress, the way you speak to and about someone, the commitment to set boundaries. There is very little respect on display today, especially to those that think differently than you. Respect goes beyond opinion and shows a sincere love for the human race. Relationships demand respect. We must respect the one we are dating enough to ask, "If another guy is dating my future wife the way I am dating my current girlfriend, am I okay with that?" or, "If another girl is dating my future husband the way I am dating my current boyfriend, am I okay with that?" This really brings respect into perspective. When you do nothing out of selfish ambition, you show great respect. Because of our selfish, fallen nature, relationships are steered more by selfish ambition than humility and respect that values others above ourselves. All relationships should set boundaries, and out of respect, you should push each other to follow those boundaries.

This chapter was written to give you some thoughts about implementing healthy guardrails in your personal life and relationships. Whether you are currently in a relationship or not, this chapter is for you.

Be wise. Be proactive. Be healthy when it comes to your relationships.

# Chapter 12

# Temptation

**FIRST THESSALONIANS 4:3–5:** "It is God's will that you should be sanctified: that you should avoid sexual immorality; that each of you should learn to control your own body in a way that is holy and honorable, not in passionate lust like the pagans, who do not know God" (NIV).

This passage starts with, "It is God's will." This does not mean that following directives are all that God's will encompasses for your life. "Clearly the need for sanctification and the specific regulations defining godly behavior given in 4:3–8 reflect one narrow segment of the 'will,' not an all-encompassing statement of it."[1] It does, however, give us standards for living that show we are following the will of God for our life. If you are not faithful in the easy times of life, then you are more than likely to be unfaithful in the difficult times.

## Purity

Paul is challenging the church of Thessalonica here in this passage to remain *pure*. The first thing we find in this passage that Paul addresses is to "avoid sexual immorality." "The word

---

[1] D. M. Martin, *1, 2 Thessalonians*, Vol. 33 (Nashville: Broadman & Holman Publishers, 1995), 121.

'immorality' (*Greek: porneia*) was used frequently in Judeo-Christian literature where it could refer to premarital or extramarital intercourse, prostitution, incest, and any other type of sexual impropriety."[2] Sexual immorality was extremely common during this era of history and in the culture surrounding the church to which Paul was writing. He wanted the church to know and grasp that living a sanctified life requires living life counter to the culture. Believers are to live by the standards of the Word of God and the conviction of the Holy Spirit, regardless of social and cultural norms. Sex is a gift from God that is intended for the marriage bed between a husband and a wife, like we discussed in the previous chapter. This means that boyfriends do not get husband privileges, nor do girlfriends get wife privileges.

One of the greatest challenges in keeping a God-centered relationship healthy is staying pure in your relationship. To have a God-centered relationship, you must move past your fleshly desires and follow God's commands regardless of the cost and regardless of whether it's relevant to what's promoted by our society. God is not trying to hold us back here or make our lives miserable; His intention in highlighting purity is to free us up! God designed sex, and sex is great when done God's way. God designed it to be a gift between one woman and one man who have made a covenant with each other and before God in marriage. The consequences of the sin of sexual immorality are like every other sin and must be dealt with by confession and repentance before the Lord. If not dealt with, it can and will create baggage in your life for the future. Marriage requires work and is hard enough without unnecessary baggage brought in. The choices you make today will determine the baggage you carry with you into tomorrow. God's Word is given to us to challenge us to live our life God's way, which in turn will free us up to live a life of hope and grace in the future.

---

[2] Ibid., 123.

## Self-Control

The next part of 1 Thessalonians 4 that I want us to look at in this chapter is verse 4, "that each of you should learn to control your own body in a way that is holy and honorable" (NIV). We see that your body is a temple of the Holy Spirit in 1 Corinthians 6:19: "Do you not know that your bodies are temples of the Holy Spirit who is in you, whom you have from God? You are not your own." "Just as the name of God dwelt in Solomon's temple (1 Kgs. 8:29; 2 Chr. 6:2), the Holy Spirit now lives and dwells in the New Testament temple which is the body of believers gathering in the name of Jesus (Matt. 18:20)."[3] We are the temple of the Holy Spirit. Through salvation, the Holy Spirit comes to live inside of us, and we are called to live out our faith.

John McArthur says about 1 Corinthians 6:19, "Paul calls for sexual purity not only because of the way sexual sin affects the body, but because the body it affects is not even the believer's own. Understanding the reality of the phrase *the Holy Spirit who is in you, whom you have from God* should give us as much commitment to purity as any knowledge of divine truth could."[4] This is the reason we should learn self-control, to control your own body in a way that is holy and honorable.

The question then lies: *How do you control your own body in a way that is holy and honorable?* This is one of the great challenges of life. We watch moral failure happen all too often as a result of a sinful decision that could have been overcome by controlling one's body. One question I get asked often as a college pastor is, "How do I handle the porn addiction in my life?" I recommend

[3] R. L. Pratt Jr., *I & II Corinthians*, Vol. 7 (Nashville, TN: Broadman & Holman Publishers, 2000), 50.

[4] John F. MacArthur, *First Corinthians: MacArthur New Testament Commentary* (Chicago, IL: Moody Publishers, 1984), 152.

over and over again the greatest way to control your body, and that simple step is with Scripture.

Hebrews 4:12 says, "For the word of God is living and effective and sharper than any double-edged sword, penetrating as far as the separation of soul and spirit, joints and marrow. It is able to judge the thoughts and intentions of the heart." God's Word penetrates. There is nothing more powerful to do with the temptation we face than fight it with Scripture. In Matthew 4:1–11, Jesus is tempted by the devil following His forty-day fast in the wilderness. During that time of temptation, He responded three different times, "It is written," referring to the Scriptures. There is no greater weapon to fight against the temptation of the world, the flesh, and the devil than the Holy Word of God. "I have stored up your word in my heart, that I might not sin against you" (Ps. 119:11 ESV).

I have seen men and women take Scripture and post it every-where they are tempted. I have seen it taped to steering wheels, posted on mirrors, in Ziplock bags in the shower, above beds, all over the walls, and the background of their phones. Why? Why would college students go to such extreme lengths not to sin? Simply because they long to control their bodies—the Spirit's temple—in such a way that is honoring and holy before the Lord.

Every believer must identify the areas in their life which are not being lived in a holy and honorable way. After you identify these areas of temptation, search for Scripture to memorize to combat that temptation. Sin should break us to the point that we desire to change. Change today and write down areas in your life that you need to adjust so you can get your life aligned with God's Word, and ask the Lord to break your heart for the things in your life that break His.

## "Not in Passionate Lust"

First Thessalonians 4:5 continues on in this thought by making the statement "not in passionate lust like the pagans, who do
not know God" (NIV). Ever since the fall of man in Genesis 3,
humanity has constantly struggled and fallen into the sins of passionate lust and immorality. We see this in Genesis 19 with the
cities of Sodom and Gomorrah. *Baker Encyclopedia of the Bible*
describes the city of Sodom this way:

> The basic story of Sodom and Gomorrah occurs
> in Genesis 18 and 19, although the biblical inter-
> est in the city begins in chapter 13 with the
> decision of Lot, Abraham's nephew, to settle in
> the Jordan Valley in the vicinity of Sodom (vv.
> 10–13), among people who were "wicked, great
> sinners against the Lord" (v. 13). It becomes clear
> (19:4, 5) that one of Sodom's most grievous sins
> was sexual perversion, especially homosexuality.
> Lot's offer of his virgin daughters to the men
> of Sodom to turn their attention away from his
> heavenly visitors is an indication of the demor-
> alizing influence of the city (v. 8). The prophet
> Ezekiel (16:49) lists pride, prosperous compla-
> cency, and "abomination" as the sins of Sodom.[5]

This was a very dark city, full of perverse and passionate
lusts of the flesh. Passionate lust has been around since the fall
of man, and it is certainly celebrated in our society. Today, the
porn industry is growing more and more powerful, elevating at
an alarming rate, simply because it has become easier and easier

---

[5] W. A. Elwell and B. J. Beitzel, "Sodom and Gomorrah" in *Baker
Encyclopedia of the Bible*, Vol. 2 (Grand Rapids, MI: Baker Book House,
1988).

to access privately. The statistics are staggering to say the least. Websites like www.xxxchurch.com are working hard to provide helpful guides to win this war, but the lust of the human race is a heart issue that can only be transformed by the redemptive work of Jesus Christ and what He accomplished on the cross.

Pornography is one of the greatest sin struggles men and women deal with today. Porn is destroying marriages, killing relationships, creating baggage, and crushing our identity. Scripture speaks to this topic often. Job said in Job 31:1, "I made a covenant with my eyes not to look lustfully at a young woman" (NIV). The author of Psalm 119 says, "How can a young man keep his way pure? By keeping your word. I have sought you with all my heart; don't let me wander from your commands. I have treasured your word in my heart so that I may not sin against you" (vv. 9–11). Paul addresses it in a big way to the Corinthians and the Church at Corinth, where many had fallen into sexual sin, along with other sins. All through the Bible you find passionate lust being addressed in one way or the other.

College students need no additional help in being tempted with lust, and our enemy, the devil, knows it. One-night stands, hooking up for fun, drunk sex, and so much more are happening daily simply to fulfill a lustful desire instead of striving to fulfill our lives with the only thing that can fill them—God. Why give away in one night what you can one day gift to your spouse for a lifetime? Lust takes that gift away.

David himself fell into this temptation in 2 Samuel 11. What you let in you will come out, like we discussed in the last chapter on GIGO. If you allow lustful images into your mind, you will pursue lustful actions. Who you follow on social media can drive the sexual desire inside of you. This is why I preach often to young ladies about the power of their clothing, and I strongly advise them to dress in such a way that is holy and honorable to the Lord. When you look in the mirror before leaving home, consider pausing and asking yourself, *Will I cause anyone to stumble? Am I making holiness easier or harder for my brothers in Christ?* Romans 14:13 says, "Therefore let us no longer judge one another. Instead decide never to put a stumbling block or pitfall in the way of your brother or sister." Don't get me wrong—if a man lusts after you, it is *his* fault and not yours. Nonetheless, Christians are called to lay down our perceived rights in order to serve the weaker among us. If a brother is weak in this area, consider how you can love and serve him by your choice of clothing. Let us not intentionally make it more difficult for one another than what it already is.

To win this war, we must join together as believers and fight. When a follower slips and stumbles, don't just walk on by—stop and pick them up. Ladies, dress for what you want to attract. We must help each other. Guys, can I encourage you to set boundaries with the ladies in your life? Have friendship boundaries, boundaries in a relationship, party boundaries, and have those around you that will hold you accountable to the boundaries you set. Work together to make it hard to fall for passionate lust. Again, this is why Christian community is SO valuable here. Those who desire to imitate Christ live in such a way that they desire to imitate Christ.

The good news is, many college students today are fighting against this battle and winning—and so can you! First John 4:4 says, "the one who is in you is greater than the one who is in the world." President Dwight Eisenhower once said, "I never saw a pessimistic general win a battle." If you believe you will fall and lose, you will! Don't believe temptation is defeating you; believe that through the power of the Holy Spirit living in you, you can overcome it.

To fight temptation you have to be willing to do whatever it takes. What extreme measures do you need to take to fight this fight? Do you need to get rid of your smartphone and go back to the simplicity of an old-school flip phone? Do you need to allow a close mentor to receive messages of everything you do online? (See www.xxxchurch.com for helpful ideas.) Do you need to get rid of some clothes and start dressing differently, more modestly, and surround yourself with different people? Do you maybe need to date someone different or not date at all for a season? Fight against temptation; don't just keep falling into it. I am very encouraged by the men and women I know personally who are passionately fighting this battle in their personal lives and who are winning. And so can you!

Temptation is defined in James 1:14 as being enticed by our own evil desires. And this enticing is something that follows every Christian around every day that we live. There are a number of things done to overcome the power of temptation, all of which are through the mighty work of the Holy Spirit. I have certainly experienced my fair share of temptation even in my short twenty years of life and I'm confident that it will continue with less and less power but will remain constant in presence until my sanctification is complete.

With all that said, I believe there are a few key points to seeing victory against temptation. First, we need to fight emphatically with the power of prayer that fully rests on God's grace in answering as shown in the Lord's Prayer (Luke 11:4; Matt. 6:13) and in Luke 22:46 when Jesus tells the disciples to "Pray, so that you will not fall into temptation." The next line of defense is that of Bible saturation. If we are going to wage a war against sin and temptation, we need to take up, as Ephesians 6:17 states, "the sword of the Spirit—which is the word of God."

I once heard Francis Chan state that the Bible carries as much authority as if we were to hear the literal voice of God in a crack of thunder. That level of power, wisdom, and sheer love is all within the Word of God just waiting to be opened up and prayerfully considered with all of its implications that allow such amazing deliverance from our evil desires. A few practical ways of applying this are in daily quiet times, transforming a space by putting Scripture around it, and memorizing large portions of Scripture.

My last piece of advice to fight temptation is to give it everything you have because it is God who works in you in the same way that Philippians 2:12–13 addresses working out our salvation. Especially when battling a very deep-rooted temptation, drastic life changes have to be made and that will be different for every person, but no matter what the trial is, know that God is faithful and will not allow us to be tempted beyond what we can bear (1 Cor. 10:13).

The reason all of this is of the upmost importance is because God is glorified in the overcoming of temptation, we are commanded all throughout Scripture to rid ourselves of the desires of the flesh, and in all of this we experience the fullness of joy found in Christ.

—Kyle Beard

# Chapter 13

# Identifying the One

IT'S PRETTY TYPICAL DURING the college years that students begin to desire to find "the one" who could be their future spouse. I will never forget my senior year of college, when I went through a breakup with a great girl. Was God playing a joke on me? I knew Matthew 6:25 told me, "Don't worry about your life," but that seemed easier said than done when it came to relationships. Then I read in Philippians 4:6: "Don't worry about anything; instead, pray about everything" (NLT). When it comes to finding "the one," we often worry about finding him or her and wonder if that person could be that "magical soul mate" more than we ever pray for him or her.

In regards to finding "the one," as it's so often dubbed in our society, a question I often get asked by young adults is, "Does God really have just *one* person out there in this world for me?" Out of the 7.5 billion people in the world, is there really just one that God has created and designed for you to spend your life with? My answer is yes; I believe that God has the story of your life written before you were even born according to Psalm 139:16. He is sovereign and trustworthy. I believe that if He has ordained your days before you were even born, and His plan is for you to be married in this life, then He also knows who that person is that you will marry. And in His sovereign way, He will bring the two of you together as you both seek after Him and His will for your life.

But I also believe that for some of you, His plan for your life doesn't necessarily include marriage. But what I hope to accomplish in this chapter is to challenge us to a different way of thinking about singleness and marriage as well as give practical wisdom and advice on how to pray for, look for, and then pursue a godly guy or girl to date with the intentions of marriage, should that be your desire.

When we find ourselves asking if there is just *one* person out there for us, I believe we're asking the wrong question. I believe it's imperative in this season of your life to focus not on finding "the one," but instead on who you are becoming, and to focus more on becoming "the one." You should take ownership in growing up and maturing, allowing the Lord to develop you into the godly man or woman that He desires for you to become, should He call you into marriage someday. When that becomes your focus, it frees you up! It allows you to let go of the pressure of questioning and evaluating every girl or guy you encounter as potential mate status and, as a result, you live free to trust in the sovereignty of God to write your story. It's from that place you can then live with peace, knowing that you have entrusted your future to the Lord, whether or not that includes finding that "special someone" to enter the next stage of life with.

*"Let him pursue you," "be submissive," "he just leads me so well," "stay pure."* This was all I knew about what a godly relationship looked like until I met the love of my life in college. Now hear me out, I am not going to sit here and give you the "how to do" a godly relationship in college because I would be lying to you. I will tell you what God has taught me through my story and some things I believe He wants me to share with you.

I met my husband in college when I least expected it. I started recklessly chasing after the Lord and actually prayed to be single. Please don't misunderstand what I am saying. There is a misconceived idea that the second you are content in your singleness you will be immediately blessed with a godly partner. That is not how our God works. He is not a machine who can be manipulated. He wants us content in Him no matter the circumstance. I got closer to this kind of contentment in Jesus. He is the only one who could satisfy me. Shortly after this time, God gave me the biggest blessing—apart from Himself—in my life. He gave me a godly man to do life with and then later called both of us to ministry.

That was just a tiny piece of my story. Here are some things I have learned throughout this process.

I have a role to play in finding a godly man. Godly men look for godly women and vice versa. I realized I have just as much responsibility to stay pure, to push my boyfriend toward purity, to spend intimate time with God, and to serve Him. I have to seek Christ with all my heart, mind, soul, and strength. This allowed me to want to seek someone who will push me toward Him. I have learned that even in a godly relationship, you will still not be fully satisfied. The Lord is the only one who will never let you down. He has shown me the joy in serving Christ with someone to love alongside me.

John 16 explains that when Jesus left the earth, He gave us a Helper. This Helper is the Holy Spirit. Ultimately, dating to honor the Lord comes from this Helper. He is the only one that will make you pure. Yes, you can have self-control and set up boundaries that direct you toward success, but without the Holy Spirit, there is no point. Another beautiful gift God has given us is the gift of other people who also have this Helper working for them. Surround yourself with these people because the more of the Holy Spirit you are encountering, the more growth you will see in your walk.

Ultimately, finding that relationship is not the climax of your story. It is an important decision and arguably one of the most important ones, but it is not where your walk stops. Your walk on earth stops when you see God face-to-face someday. Surrender every part of your life. Your relationships, your job, your location, your everything. This is when you experience things only God can do. Not just things you think up or imagine, but bigger than something you could ever fathom yourself. Lamentations 3:23 says that His mercies are made new every morning, so live like it.

—Alex Lunsion, junior, University of Arkansas

## Singleness Isn't Second Best

When you pursue a relationship with the intentions of marriage, it is a great thing. Marriage is beautiful. God designed the covenant of marriage in Genesis 2 between a man and women as an earthly gift this side of heaven. But God has a plan for each and every one of us, and for some, that won't include marriage. He's got this, so pray, talk to Him, and surrender it to Him, ultimately leaving the outcome of your future in His capable hands.

I want to challenge you to think differently when it comes to the idea of singleness and relationships. While the Bible is clear that marriage is wonderful, it is also clear that not all people will get married, and that there are some wonderful and unique benefits to being single.

Just look at the life of the apostle Paul and the impact he made on this world for the gospel of Jesus Christ. Singleness can be a scary word in our churches today, but it shouldn't be; it is a beautiful gift, as Paul describes it in 1 Corinthians 7. Yes, so much of our society is centered around couples, marriage, and family, but we've got to move beyond the enemy's lie in believing that singleness is "second best." If you are single as you read this section, please don't get lost in a negative view of singleness and miss the purpose and blessing that God can have waiting for you there. You must remember that singleness is a gift, just as marriage is a gift.

This is where letting go and letting God be the author of His story for your life can be freeing. Being single frees you up to be fully devoted and undivided to kingdom things without the distractions and obligations that having a spouse and a family can add to your life.

For those who would like to be married and don't believe right now that God is calling you to singleness, I want to share with you some wisdom regarding how you might go about finding a spouse.

### Step 1: Pray

While you wait and as you may be discerning if marriage is what the Lord has for your future, pray. Like I mentioned earlier, we question, worry, and wonder about the potential of a person or a relationship, but are we taking intentional time to pray about this potential next season of our life? The first step I want to challenge you to do in preparing yourself for your potential spouse is to pray for him or her.

Have you ever written down a prayer list of specifics to begin praying now for your future spouse? Come up with a list of what I like to call the "negotiables and the non-negotiables," which are qualities and characteristics of a person you hope to find someday. Pray through those. Pray for them even though you might not know your future spouse's name yet. You might not know their height, their hair color, or any other feature, but be prayerful that one day you will meet someone God has chosen for you to spend the rest of your life with.

Remember Philippians 4:6? "Don't worry about anything; instead, pray about everything" (NLT). Worry will never get you closer to finding your spouse, but prayer can. Commit today to begin praying for your future spouse, even if you don't know their name.

Here are a few things to add to your prayer list:

1. Pray for their purity.

   "Therefore, put to death what belongs to your earthly nature: sexual immorality, impurity, lust, evil desire, and greed, which is idolatry." (Col. 3:5)

2. Pray for God to guard their heart in the waiting.

   "Guard your heart above all else, for it is the source of life." (Prov. 4:23)

3. Pray God's armor of protection over them daily, that they will stand strong against the devil's evil schemes.

   "For our struggle is not against flesh and blood, but against the rulers, against the authorities, against the cosmic powers of this darkness, against evil, spiritual forces in the heavens." (Eph. 6:12)

4. Pray that they are becoming more disciplined in their spiritual life so they can sharpen you spiritually.

   "Iron sharpens iron, and one person sharpens another." (Prov. 27:17)

5. Pray for wisdom.

   "Blessed are those who find wisdom, those who gain understanding." (Prov. 3:13 NIV)

6. Pray that God in Christ is making them blameless and pure.

   "So that you may be blameless and pure, children of God who are faultless in a crooked and perverted generation, among whom you shine like stars in the world." (Phil. 2:15)

7. Pray for blessing and the favor of God over them daily.

   "Never let loyalty and faithfulness leave you. Tie them around your neck; write them on the tablet of your heart. Then you will find favor and high regard with God and people." (Prov. 3:3–4)

8. Pray your spouse has a hunger for God's Word.

"How sweet your word is to my taste—sweeter than honey in my mouth." (Ps. 119:103)

### Step 2: Keep Your Eyes Open

Once you have created a prayer list and are praying for the possibility of a relationship with a potential someone who lines up with your list of "negotiables and non-negotiables," keep your eyes open for that person who catches your attention. We've talked a lot about wisdom in this book, and one of the most important areas to apply godly wisdom in your life is in the pursuit of a spouse. There are several things you should look for in a potential husband or wife, and several things you should look out for. I want to help you consider some ways you can prepare for marriage and what to look for in a potential godly husband or wife.

The first step in finding a spouse is to seek God with all your heart. Too many believers are trying to find love in all the wrong places. If you are seeking after God with all you are and your future spouse is doing the same, you may look up one day and find them running alongside you as you both are pursuing Christ. Your focus is not primarily on seeking the next relationship, but on seeking after the only real, fulfilling relationship there is—your personal relationship with Jesus Christ Himself. This is where you must start when looking for a spouse.

"Do not be yoked together with unbelievers. For what do righteousness and wickedness have in common? Or what fellowship can light have with darkness?" (2 Cor. 6:14 NIV). The Bible makes it pretty clear that Christians should not marry—and thus, should not date—people who are not Christians. This would bring far too much relational chaos, and would misrepresent the relationship of Christ and His church, to which marriage is meant to point.

As you're chasing after Christ, your character will be shaped more and more. Your character should be more attractive on the inside than your looks are on the outside. We have a tendency to prioritize and chase after physical attractiveness and appearance over godliness and the character of the heart. Don't get me wrong—it's good to be attracted to someone you'd like to potentially marry. But physical attraction should never trump godliness. "Don't let your beauty consist of outward things like elaborate hairstyles and wearing gold jewelry or fine clothes, but rather what is inside the heart—the imperishable quality of a gentle and quiet spirit, which is of great worth in God's sight" (1 Pet. 3:3–4).

I don't think there is a better illustration of this pursuit than "the relationship triangle."

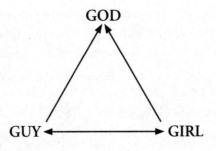

Don't compromise when it comes to a guy or a girl having potential. Never allow charm to trump godliness. Proverbs 31:30 says, "Charm is deceptive and beauty is fleeting, but a woman who fears the LORD will be praised." Men and women in a relationship should stay true to their convictions. Never compromise on this. What you should hope and pray for is both character and charm. When your priorities change as you are looking for potential in a guy or a girl, so will your view of relationships.

Dating. Something that is fun and awesome. Something that a lot of people dream about doing perfectly. Something that is defined as a stage of romantic relationships in humans whereby two people meet socially with the aim of each assessing the other's suitability as a prospective partner in marriage. Something that everyone seems to think is going to fulfill their every need.

Despite all of the good intentions, dating can't fulfill these things. In fact, many times, dating leads to pain and heartache that shakes people to their core. This occurs when one or both parties in the relationship puts their hope and trust in one another as opposed to putting them in the One who deserves that honor—Jesus Christ.

I want to give you practical steps that will help you not only date in a more God-centered way, but also encourage you in your walk as a whole.

1. Pick and Pursue the Godly: This is one of the most important pieces of how to date in a godly way. Many of you may ask, *How do I do this, because it sounds simple in statement but is difficult in application?* One big nugget of information here is you must first look deeper than what you can see on the surface. Early in my life when I was much less mature in my faith, I wanted a relationship so badly, but I wanted it for all the wrong reasons. I wanted a girl that my friends would look at and then affirm me that she was super attractive or insanely cool. I was so caught up in seeking the approval of others in my love life that I lost sight of what God had intended for me and my relationship. It wasn't until I really started looking for a girl who would push me to be a better, more Christlike guy that I was blessed with a girl who would be my eventual wife. Not only was this girl a solid girl that made me pursue Jesus at an even faster pace, she was everything I could ever want in a girl. God has a crazy way of working things out for those who love and trust Him, and I have seen that firsthand in my life.

2. Let Go and Let God: This phrase is one that is simple, easy to understand, and also very important. Everyone longs for a relationship so badly that it sometimes clouds their judgment. Bottom line: when you are ready for a relationship and trust God fully with your

life, He will provide for you. Philippians 4:19 says, "And my God will supply all your needs according to his riches in glory in Christ Jesus." This is a well-known verse, but do you really take it to heart? Do you truly believe it in the scope of relationships? This is a super encouraging verse and I believe wholeheartedly that it is applicable to relationships. We all know how loving and merciful our God is but, as faithful followers, it is infinitely important that we trust Him with something as crucial as our relationship with our eventual spouse.

—Jeremy Gackle, University of Arkansas student

### Step 3: Pursue

When you have identified someone and believe you could spend your life with that person, then you should pursue them. Through the pursuit stage and through prayer, you determine if this could be "the one" for you. I mentioned in the opening section of this chapter that we must get lost in the intimate pursuit of God daily, and if that pursuit brings us to an opportunity to pursue a potential spouse, then you must pursue them with godly intentions. Always remember, you will only date *whom* you pursue and you will also date *the way* you pursue. Follow me here—you would never go to a local Mexican food restaurant to get a great cup of coffee. No, you'd seek out and go to the best coffee shop in your town to find exactly what you're looking for. To identify "the one" whom God might have for you, you must first identify the godly. Or to say it more simply, to identify the *potential* of "the one," you must identify the godly in your life.

If you've found another godly person chasing Jesus right beside you, you may be ready to pursue a relationship with this person. You're not yet at the "commitment stage," but the stage that leads you toward entering into a commitment. You're dating, not aimlessly, but with the purpose and intentions of finding a spouse and the person to spend the rest of your life with.

We tend to put a lot of pressure on this stage, but hear me say this—one date *does not* equal marriage, so don't hold that pressure over some poor guy or girl. One date shows interest and potential, but could end by the end of that date. Never read too much into one initial date. Just because you might date someone that you find to be godly and they might have great potential, you may come to realize that you're not compatible with that person—that is okay. This is normal and does not mean you're out of track with God; it simply means they are just not "the one" for you.

## Learn to Identify Spiritual Fruit

The fruit or evidence of an individual's spiritual life should come through in the way they live. Are you seeking to pursue someone that is producing godly fruit? Are you saying yes to someone that lives out a godly pursuit in his or her personal life, spiritually speaking? John the Baptist came down pretty hard on this idea of bearing fruit, saying in Matthew 3:10, "Even now the ax of God's judgment is poised, ready to sever the roots of the trees. Yes, every tree that does not produce good fruit will be chopped down and thrown into the fire" (NLT).

The one we seek to pursue should be producing godly fruit. If they just attend church and straighten up their life simply in order to date you, then there is a good chance you will compromise and will stop going to church together once they have convinced you to date them. Remember, it is easier to pull someone down than to pull someone up. Pursue the godly to get the godly. If you have to change them, don't pursue them. Pursuing the godly does not free you from sin, but it does put people together with the same standards, principles, and convictions. The godly still sin and so will you. Never put yourself above any sin. Live your life with convictions and boundaries when it comes to your relationships. Once a relationship turns physical it takes the relationship emotionally into levels you might not be ready for. Never understatement the power of physical touch in a relationship. Set boundaries and protect yourself.

Clear communication with each other and guidance from the Holy Spirit living within you should guide you to this point, not physical attraction. Physical attraction is important but through clear communication you find out if you are compatible. All males and females are compatible physically, God designed it that way, but that does not mean we are all meant to be sexually intimate. Communication is the greatest key to a successful relationship. If you can't communicate, you can't function in a relationship. Communication might be one of the hardest things to learn, and there are many great books out there about it. We will not take time to cover it in this book, but when it comes to your relationship I highly suggest you read more on the power of communication in relationships. Through communication during the pursuit stage, you may come to find a desire to commit to each other and become a "couple."

The commitment stage is to determine if the "one" you have found is "the one" for you. During this stage you should have great peace in your prayer life and in your personal time with the Lord that you have found "the one" and feel completely at peace in moving forward with a forever commitment with this individual. However, it is with great compassion that I share with you in this book, that if you don't have peace, I encourage you to step back, break up, and take a break to evaluate your own personal walks with Christ and the future direction of your relationship. Never rush the commitment stage. Sometimes it means taking a break, stepping back, doing life together as friends, and then seeing where it takes you.

In closing, I just want to remind you that finding a spouse in college shouldn't be your end goal. It is completely okay to not even enter this stage or to rush into dating. Singleness is a blessing and there is nothing wrong with it. Don't let the world, your friends, or your family push you to rushing into a relationship that you are not ready for or that you don't long to be in. When you rush God's plan for your life, it then becomes your plan and no longer God's plan. College is a time where the reality of marriage might come alive, but don't rush into any relationship simply with the hopes to get married. Remember to use this season of your life to grow, mature, and deepen your walk with the Lord. Be content with where God has you and allow Him the freedom to develop you to become the person that He desires for you to become, regardless of any relationship.

One of my favorite verses is Matthew 6:33–34. It says, "Seek first the kingdom of God and his righteousness, and all these things will be provided for you. Therefore don't worry about tomorrow, because tomorrow will worry about itself. Each day has enough trouble of its own." Seek first what God wants for you, not just what you want. Everyone has dreams and ideals about their future, but those may be your desires and not God's. So seek Him first, and allow Him to guide your steps. Stop worrying and start seeking Him through prayer.

# Part 6

# A Foundation for Success

## Chapter 14

# The Value of Hard Work

**WORK . . . SOME PEOPLE** hate it, some people love it. Some people go to great lengths to avoid it, while others become workaholics. One thing I have learned about work is that, regardless of how much you enjoy it, it must be done. One of the greatest life lessons you can learn young is the *value* of hard work. My parents taught me the value of hard work as a kid, and I think it was one of the greatest things that they instilled in me. Understanding the value of hard work will take you from being just an average college student to an exceptional college student.

This is a value that can and will launch you into your future if you apply a hard work ethic in your daily life. We must have a greater desire within us than just playing video games, goofing around with friends, or eating junk food. The drive within us will determine the effort we put forth.

Champions are not made in the gym; they are made by how hard they work in the gym. You can stand in a gym as long as you want, but unless you're working, you won't accomplish anything. Those who work hard in the gym don't have to post about it on social media; it's simply noticed by the results. Hard work comes by saying no to laziness in life, and saying yes to discipline. To win in college you must brace yourself for the impact and get to work.

## Work Wholeheartedly

All throughout Scripture, God has given us a clear perspective about work ethic. For instance, take what King Solomon said in Ecclesiastes 2:24–25, "There is nothing better for a person than to eat, drink, and enjoy his work. I have seen that even this is from God's hand, because who can eat and who can enjoy life apart from him?" He is simply stating here that we can find great satisfaction in our work. We all long to live within our passions and desires, and there is a place for that within the work ethic of your life. There are times when God is going to take you through a season of development. In these seasons, you may not be living right in your passion or your ultimate heart's desire, but they are necessary for your development and spiritual maturity, and you have to trust God's reasoning for the process. Finding satisfaction where you are in every season means you must make the most of every opportunity.

Paul challenged the church in Colossae with this concept. In Colossians 3, Paul gives instructions to the household. In verse 22 he says, "Slaves, obey your human masters in everything. Don't work only while being watched, as people-pleasers, but work wholeheartedly, fearing the Lord." Paul says to "work wholeheartedly." No matter what work you're doing, whether it is seen by people or not, do it with all your heart.

There will be times in college, as well as in life after college, when you will not want to give 100 percent. It is in those times where you must still push yourself to work "wholeheartedly." Wholehearted work is disciplined worked. It is the weight room and the unseen moments of life where we must work without being seen, without recognition. We do this because we know that the Lord sees and we work hard to honor Him. Those of you who work out know it is not always easy to motivate yourself for that day's workout—especially when you are still sore from the day before. But it is in those moments that you must make a decision to be disciplined.

Remember Proverbs 6:9–11: "How long will you stay in bed, you slacker? When will you get up from your sleep? A little sleep, a little slumber, a little folding of the arms to rest, and your poverty will come like a robber, your need, like a bandit." We can't allow laziness to slip in and keep us from being all that God intends for us to be. God expects us to be our best at all we do and to do it "wholeheartedly." There will be many times when you will desire to set down the books, sleep in, skip out on your job, or not get all of your community service hours in for that program because you are tired or you feel you deserve some "me time." Proverbs 12:11 says the opposite of this mind-set: "The one who works his land will have plenty of food, but whoever chases fantasies lacks sense." Don't chase after your fantasies; be present, and live in the reality of the responsibilities of your day. Sometimes what you want to do, you should not do, even though you may desire to do it.

My story doesn't begin at the University of Arkansas, but starts in my senior year of high school. All throughout high school, I was recruited to play D1 football. Unfortunately, my senior year I became plagued with injury after injury. My dad had invested so much time, effort, and money into my football career for it just to fizzle out. My senior year of high school, I may have lost football, but in this struggle, Jesus found me and radically changed my life on October 17, 2014.

With losing the chance to play collegiate football and my dad having invested so much in my pursuit of football, this led to me having to pay for my college education. With me having to pay, the best option would be to go to community college my first year and then transfer to the University of Arkansas. In this transfer process I would meet my mentor, pastor, and great friend, Brian Mills, who has asked me to give you some advice on work ethic, and here's what the Lord has put on my heart.

First, Proverbs 14:23: "All hard work brings a profit, but mere talk leads only to poverty" (NIV). You must walk the walk; you cannot just talk the talk. In whatever you do, do it to glorify the Lord and recognize that the small things matter. Go a mile deep, and not a mile wide in everything that you do. College is hard, work is hard, but hard work brings profit and the Lord always knows and sees your hard work. He sees everything that you do, even when no one is around.

Second, Isaiah 14:3: "When the LORD gives you rest from your pain, torment, and the hard labor you were forced to do . . ." This verse is encouraging because it's saying after your hard work and your struggles, you will take up a taunt, given by the Lord, to call out your demons and your struggles, laying your stake with Jesus. It is critical to know that when life gets hard and it seems like you can't do anything, take rest in the Lord, knowing that you were meant to serve that hard labor.

Last, Isaiah 49:2: "He made my words like a sharp sword; he hid me in the shadow of his hand. He made me like a sharpened arrow; he hid me in his quiver." Know that in everything you are doing, no matter how hard it is, the Lord is sharpening you, every single day of your life. He is seeking you, finding you, and standing with you in every second of every day.

I'm not going to lie, college can be difficult, especially when you are trying to serve and work at the same time. However, I have the key to success in this, and it's JESUS. He will carry you and mold you into the young adult that He has called you to be. These verses have helped me through these trials, and hopefully the Lord uses them to help you as well.

—Daniel Cole, junior, University of Arkansas

We learn the concept of work from the very beginning in Genesis 2:15: "The LORD God took the man and placed him in the garden of Eden to work it and watch over it." This is a pre-fall theology of work, a picture of work before sin entered the world. Then we see after the fall of man in Genesis 3, when sin entered the world, the concept of work has now been corrupted. Work is now frustrating and less fruitful than it was first intended to be. In Genesis 3:19, we read, "You will eat bread by the sweat of your brow until you return to the ground, since you were taken from it. For you are dust, and you will return to dust." This is a picture of the frustration attached to work in a post-fall world.

God intends for humans to work as long as they live. Work calls for obedience, even when it seems that no one else is watching. Even if it seems that the professor isn't paying attention, a good student is consistent and diligent to the task at hand. God intends for us to work, and work should bring meaning to our lives. It should give us a sense of purpose. To fulfill this call, you must have the right perspective about work, because work is not a punishment or a penalty but a blessing. It should give us great fulfillment in life when we work hard for something and then see the fruit of our labor.

Our society has the wrong perspective of work, and as a result, many of us have an entitled vision of work and life. God has given us each gifts, talents, and desires, and these are to be used to expand His kingdom. As we seek to put them into practice, we can pray that God will bless us with a job opportunity that will put His glory on display and be helpful to people. Even if it's not necessarily the job we dreamed of or hoped to end up with, it's a job we've been blessed with.

## What We Learn from Nehemiah

Let's take a quick look at the life of Nehemiah. He was a cupbearer to the king. Now that was a pretty impressive job, but God had given him a greater vision. But if Nehemiah had not been the best cupbearer that he could be in that season of his life, then he would not have had received the favor of the king, which was critical to then be able to pursue the passion and vision that God had put on his heart.

Paul understood the power of making the most of where you are when he told the church at Colossae in Colossians 3:23–24, "Whatever you do, do it from the heart, as something done for the Lord and not for people, knowing that you will receive the reward of an inheritance from the Lord. You serve the Lord Christ."

We must stop feeling defeated by what we don't have, or discouraged by what we don't get to do in the moment. We should instead recognize what we do have and work at it with all of our heart as if working for the Lord. This is what Nehemiah did, and the result was that he gained favor with the king, which God used to give Nehemiah a true dream job. We must utilize the gifts and talents that God has given us in the present moment of life, regardless of our circumstances.

Live faithfully and allow the Lord to be the one to do your promoting, rather than selfishly pursuing just your wants and your desires.

As we wrap up this chapter, let me give you some advice. Just pretend we are at your local coffee shop and this would be some advice that I give all of the students who I meet with. Grab your pen and notebook and jot these down so you can take them with you in the next stages of your life.

### 1. Your attitude affects your altitude.

"Do everything without grumbling and arguing, so that you may be blameless and pure, children of God who are faultless in a crooked and perverted generation, among whom you shine like stars in the world" (Phil. 2:14–15).

People will pay attention to how you respond, and it will determine how they respond to you. Your attitude will affect your success level.

## 2. Do everything with excellence, no matter what you are doing.

"Don't work only while being watched, as people-pleasers, but as slaves of Christ, do God's will from your heart. Serve with a good attitude, as to the Lord and not to people" (Eph. 6:6–7).

Excellence is accomplished through great discipline in the life of a believer. Excellence is pursued even when no one is looking. Excellence never takes shortcuts. Those who live their life with the desire for excellence will live a life of holiness.

## 3. Work provides an opportunity for you to be Christ to all people so some may come to know Him.

"Although I am free from all and not anyone's slave, I have made myself a slave to everyone, in order to win more people. To the Jews I became like a Jew, to win Jews; to those under the law, like one under the law—though I myself am not under the law—to win those under the law. To those who are without the law, like one without the law—though I am not without God's law but under the law of Christ—to win those without the law. To the weak I became weak, in order to win the weak. I have become all things to all people, so that I may by every possible means save some. Now I do all this because of the gospel, so that I may share in the blessings" (1 Cor. 9:19–23).

Never forget that God is sovereign and He has placed you where He has you on purpose—even if you're in a difficult season. There are no accidents or mishaps with the Lord; everything He does is on purpose. Are you living your life with purpose, or are you wishing you were somewhere else or someone else? Think about Shadrach, Meshach, and Abednego in Daniel 3. They ended up in a fiery furnace due to their commitment to the Lord. Their obedience to God led them to face the furnace, and it was God who allowed them to be there. But it was for a bigger purpose! You see, we don't see God show up in this story until these three men are actually in the furnace, amongst the flames, in Daniel 3:25.

Maybe God has put you in that miserable situation that you may currently be facing for a greater purpose. Don't miss the purpose because you're more focused on yourself than on living faithfully to your God. Remember, college student, God has you right where He wants you and He will be with you through it. Your job is to remain faithful to Him in all circumstances, so that you may be able to win others to Christ by your example. Live your life with a greater purpose and end goal in mind—eternity. Set the example for others in the way you live your life, so many people may come to notice the difference in you, which is Jesus Christ.

### 4. Place yourself around competitive people if you want to push yourself to be better.

"The one who walks with the wise will become wise, but a companion of fools will suffer harm" (Prov. 13:20).

We have all heard it said that you become like the people you hang out with. This statement is true. Surround yourself with those who will sharpen you and push you to be a better you. When applying for internships, pick places that are in your area of study and choose somewhere where people are succeeding. If weighing opportunities, never say someone's "no" for them. Ask! Even if you don't feel like you could get the job, at least try! Read leadership books, and books that push you in the field you're studying, and even outside the field you're studying. Look for the highest capacity leaders in your area and email them to see if they would give you thirty minutes of their time, simply for you to go in and ask them questions. *What if they say yes?* You will need connections one day. Get connected in a local church and find godly, great leaders to mentor you and pour into you while you are in college. Use this time while you're in college to grow, develop, and become a better you. Don't allow the "college experience" to rob you of endless possibilities and opportunities to become a better you. God has a plan for you, and sadly so does the world. Which one will you pick?

### 5. When you fail, fail forward.

"My flesh and my heart may fail, but God is the strength of my heart, my portion forever" (Ps. 73:26).

Failure can be a part of success. Never let your failures define you; let them train you and use them for motivation in moving forward in your life. Some of you are letting yourselves be defined by your failures simply because you *feel* like a failure. But hear me today—God does not view you this way, nor should you view yourself this way. Return to Christ. Yes, it will take great work and effort on your part, but discipline yourself to be a faithful follower of Christ. Put yourself around the right people and move forward in your walk with Christ.

### 6. Have a purpose that is bigger than yourself.

"Let the favor of the Lord our God be on us; establish for us the work of our hands—establish the work of our hands!" (Ps. 90:17).

This is a prayer I have on my daily prayer list. I pray daily that the Lord will bless the work of my hands. Why do I pray this daily? Because, I simply want God to take hold of the tasks that He has blessed me with for the day and use them for God-sized things. Remember, it is all about your perspective! Accept the task you have been given and do it with all your heart and trust God to shine His favor on it. When you receive the favor of God on your current calling, you will experience a purpose bigger than yourself.

That is my pep talk for you today!

# Chapter 15

# Trial and Error

**AT THIS POINT IN** your life, you have probably walked through a valley or two, some of you more than others. You will often hear life described like a "roller coaster." There are times in your life where you will be on top of the mountain, so to speak, and the view from the top is absolutely spectacular. You may feel confident and in control about life and the circumstances around you. Then life takes some twists and—this could happen overnight. You may then feel like you've fallen off a cliff and are at the bottom of a mountain, not knowing which way to go or which way to turn. You feel as if everyone, including God, is against you, and you just want to quit and throw in the towel because you don't feel you have what it takes to get back up the mountain once again. You may find yourself going through a bad breakup or a failing grade; maybe you are told your parents are getting a divorce, or a loved one passes away or is diagnosed with a terminal illness; friends may turn on you and betray your trust, and so much more. The result? You feel like you can't do this anymore.

## Valley Moments

I want to help you in this chapter look at how to rejoice in the wins in life and how to deal with the losses in life. Every team eventually loses a game, but it is how they respond to that loss

161

that says a lot about that team and its future. Never feel like you are alone in this journey through life. There is not a character that we read about in Scripture that did not have low moments, but we always see that God was right there with them through it all. Just look at Moses who murdered a man and fled to the desert where he lived for forty years before God called him to confront Pharaoh and demand he let God's people go. We even see Moses debating with the Lord about how unqualified he is for the task at hand, and that God needs to choose someone else. He was living in his "valley moment."

David was anointed by Samuel to be the next king of Israel after King Saul, but after his anointing he was sent back out to the field to be a shepherd boy again until the time was right. His "valley moment" was necessary in order for God to complete the development process in him, in order for him to move forward with what the Lord had for him next. Once he became successful in the season the Lord placed him in, we find him in King Saul's house—serving him as his right-hand man, still knowing he had been anointed years earlier to be the next king, yet faithful where God had him in the present. King Saul's jealousy of David pushed him to pursue David to take his life. The story of King David and his journey to actually become king is extremely inspiring because it definitely didn't come easy to him. It was his valley moments that developed him.

Then, there is the apostle Paul, and we read about all that he had endured in his gospel ministry in 2 Corinthians 11:23–28. Paul was put in prison multiple times, and it was from prison that he wrote a good portion of the New Testament. These were all valley moments that developed him. I could go on and on through the Old and New Testaments of each character in the Bible and how they all had valley moments throughout their lives.

The point of all this is that we all walk through them, so don't feel like you're alone in yours. God gives us trials to develop us, not to destroy us. He wants to strengthen us so that we can live to the fullest in His calling on our life and fulfilling the Great Commission. God knows every day of our lives, and has a plan for our days and He knows exactly how we must be developed by them for what's to come.

You will not always live on the mountaintops in life. There will be moments when you will walk through the hard moments, through your valley season—and when you do, it will be painful. But God will always use our failures and even our low moments in order to shape us for our future, if we allow Him.

> We can rejoice, too, when we run into problems and trials, for we know that they help us develop endurance. And endurance develops strength of character, and character strengthens our confident hope of salvation. And this hope will not lead to disappointment. For we know how dearly God loves us, because he has given us the Holy Spirit to fill our hearts with his love." (Rom. 5:3–5 NLT)

The Bible tells us we must keep the valleys in perspective. This is why Solomon penned Proverbs 3:5–6: "Trust in the LORD with all your heart, and do not rely on your own understanding; in all your ways know him, and he will make your paths straight." He understood that we will face valleys and we must trust that God has everything in control, even in those moments.

What is it you need to trust the Lord has today? Let's look back at Romans 5:3, "We can rejoice." When you look at life through the lens of God's goodness and His sovereignty, you can rejoice! Paul understood this. The early church needed to be taught this due to the intense persecution they were facing. Some of you reading this book need to memorize Romans 5:3 simply for the phrase, "We can rejoice."

When you break up with the one whom you thought you would marry, you can rejoice, because God is in control. When you feel like you have let down everyone who believes in you, you can rejoice, because God is in control. When you are at the bottom and depression has grabbed a hold of you, you can rejoice, because God is still in control. You say, *How?* Let's keep reading Romans 5, and read it slow. "We can rejoice, too, when we run into problems and trials, for we know that they help us develop endurance" (v. 3 NLT): Trials produce endurance in us. They develop us. They make us more like Jesus.

## Responding to Setbacks

*Harvard Business Review* wrote an article titled "Building Resilience" in which they covered the theory of mental toughness. I would like to change the idea of mental toughness to spiritual toughness. We must become spiritually strong in order to handle the spiritual battle we are under today. Martin E. P. Seligman says in this article, "Failure is a nearly inevitable part of work; and along with dashed romance, it is one of life's most common traumas. . . . We discovered that people who don't give up have a habit of interpreting setbacks as temporary, local, and changeable."[1]

We will all face setbacks, we will face trials, we will face valleys—that is a fact—but the question we must ask ourselves is: *Will they overtake us or will we overcome them?* The answer to that can show our spiritual toughness. How do those who walk through the valleys of life find joy? They have developed their faith to the point where the JOY of the Lord truly is their strength (Neh. 8:10) . . . period! When we place our joy in what is around us or in the successes of life, we will always end disappointed, because all those things are temporary. Jesus Himself tells us in

---

[1] https://hbr.org/2011/04/building-resilience?utm_source=Brilliant%3A+The+New+Science+of+Smart+Newsletter&utm_campaign=2730ffa77a-Brilliant_Report_16_1_2012&utm_medium=email&utm_term=0_9c734401c1-2730ffa77a-306129765

John 16:33 that "in this world [we] will have trouble . . " (NIV). It's a guarantee this side of heaven.

We see this again through the life of David in Psalm 51, when he is confessing his sin to the Lord. He says in verse 12, "Restore the joy of your salvation to me." He had lost his joy because of the sin of his past that hadn't yet been dealt with. He had come before the Lord in Psalm 51 and he was asking the Lord to restore his joy. You have this same choice every day. You can learn the life lesson of the day, or you can let the life lesson defeat you. This season of your life in college will be full of life lessons. The questions for you will be, will you learn from them and allow them to develop you and make you better, producing endurance, or will you just do life and hope to figure it out day by day?

## Reflect Daily

We have discussed in previous chapters about how you learn not just from your experiences, but by *reflecting* on your experiences. You can experience life and yet never learn from it. Part of maturity comes from reflection.

The most practical and simple way to reflect on your life experiences is to keep a journal. As you walk through life and deal with different seasons of life, both the good and the bad, write down daily what you walk through and what lessons you learned through that experience. It doesn't have to be lengthy, but it will cause your mind and your heart to process what you are experiencing and grow from it.

Writing down lessons learned is reflecting, and reflecting leads to maturity. You will be confronted with a lot of extremes in college, and it's how you handle these extremes that will say a lot about you as a person, and most important, as a follower of Christ. Some of you may initially fall short by choosing worldliness over holiness. If you have already made that choice, I challenge you to stop and write down that experience, then write down lessons you have learned from it. Reflect on how your choice may have affected your reputation or relationships with those closest to you.

Learning to reflect on the choices you make will help grow you and guide you through making wiser choices in the future and will help keep you from entering unnecessary valleys.

> Do not let sin control the way you live; do not give in to sinful desires. Do not let any part of your body become an instrument of evil to serve sin. Instead, give yourselves completely to God, for you were dead, but now you have new life. So use your whole body as an instrument to do what is right for the glory of God. Sin is no longer your master, for you no longer live under the requirements of the law. Instead, you live under the freedom of God's grace. (Rom. 6:12–14 NLT)

## Today's Choices Lead to Future Freedom or Future Baggage

The valleys we walk through in life are often a result of the choices we have made. Of course, this isn't always the case. Often, suffering comes upon us that is completely outside of our control—someone gets sick, someone sins against us, tragedy strikes. But in the end, we reap what we sow. Those who make a choice to live holy lives will still have trials to walk through (just read the book of Job), yet ultimately they experience freedom in their conscience and in their emotions. Those who make poor decisions end up feeling empty, broken, and full of baggage to carry with them into their future.

Today's choices lead to either future freedom or future baggage. I have sat across a table from many college students who during their freshman year fell for the temptations of parties, alcohol, sex, and drugs. And as a result, this presented greater pressure on them, and for many of them, it pushed them into a dark and depressed state or into a hopeless mind-set. This baggage can weigh heavy on your soul and is a burden to carry around with you throughout your life. But it can be avoided by being proactive in your decision-making throughout your college years. Baggage can grow and develop over the years if never dealt with or given over to the Lord. It is a result of those experiences that we never confess to the Lord and repent of.

Repentance means to change your mind and, as a result, turn from something and move forward in the opposite direction. *Repentance* is a word we tend to run from in today's culture, but it is a word that should drive us toward deeper intimacy with our heavenly Father. Too many people are carrying around the baggage of their past, simply because they have not repented of it and given it over to the Lord. When you give it over to the Lord through repentance, you experience freedom and it changes you! Repentance drives change! "Therefore repent and turn back, so that your sins may be wiped out" (Acts 3:19).

## Failure Can Propel You Forward or Destroy You

Have you ever been around a toddler who is learning to walk? Toddlers learn to walk by falling down over, and over, and over again. What if when you were a toddler learning to walk, every time you fell down you were told to never get up and try again? To just stay there, lay there, and cry! Sad, right? Somewhere in life as we are growing and developing, we stop learning from the lessons of life, and as a result, we live our lives defeated by our failures instead of getting back up, growing, and moving forward. It is through our failures that we can find our greatest success. Growth is a positive thing, even if sometimes our growth is attained by walking through pain and failures.

We see this play out in many modern-day people. Michael Jordan, the greatest basketball player of all time, in my opinion, once said, "I've missed more than 9,000 shots in my career. I've lost almost 300 games. Twenty-six times, I've been trusted to take the game winning shot and missed. I've failed over and over and over again in my life. And that is why I succeed."[2]

Another great man who walked through failure was Walt Disney, who was fired from his newspaper job for a lack of good ideas. In 1899, Henry Ford, founder of Ford Motor Company, left his long-term, comfortable job to establish the Detroit Automobile Company with $150,000 of investor money, but only a year later, it went bankrupt.[3] The Beatles were initially turned down by almost every record label. In one infamous rejection, an executive at Decca Records declined to sign them because "guitar groups are on the way out" and they were told "The Beatles have no future in show business."[4]

Just look at one of the greatest presidents of all time, Abraham Lincoln, who in 1832 lost his job and was defeated for state legislature, in 1833 failed in business, in 1836 had a nervous breakdown, in 1838 was defeated for Speaker then lost re-nomination for US Congress, in 1849 was rejected for land officer, in 1854 was defeated in US Senate election, in 1856 was defeated for nomination for vice president, and in 1858 was once again defeated for US Senate. But Lincoln never gave up. He kept at it, and in 1860, he was elected to be the sixteenth president of the United States of America.[5]

---

[2] https://www.businessinsider.com/michael-jordan-success-2011-11

[3] https://www.history.com/this-day-in-history/henry-ford-leaves-edison -to-start-automobile-company

[4] http://www.legacy.com/news/celebrity-deaths/article/beatle-number -five-brian-epstein

[5] http://www.abrahamlincolnonline.org/lincoln/education/failures.htm

Never allow the failures in life to cause you to give up and throw in the towel. If you will learn from it, failure can propel you forward with greater momentum than before you fell. I love what a hero of mine wrote right before terminal cancer took his life at the age of fifty-one. David Landrith was my pastor, my friend, my leader at that time, and will always be one of the greatest men and greatest leaders I've ever known. He pastored Long Hollow Baptist Church in Hendersonville, Tennessee, where he kept a blog called "Doing Life Together." His last blog post was called "Forward Motion," and he penned these words:

> In life, you have to keep moving. The tendency to get stuck is part of the human equation. When we get stuck, often times we just accept it and settle in to that as our "new normal." Someone said a rut is a grave with both ends kicked out. Don't take getting stuck lying down. Try something new. Shake up your routine. If you keep doing what you're doing you'll get the same results.
>
> Bill Hybels talks about the need to "crash through quitting points." That's a good mind-set when we get stuck. Forward motion is the key. Keep moving, growing, developing, and becoming all God intends for you to be![6]

John Maxwell wrote in his book *Failing Forward*, "In life, the question is not if you will have problems, but how you are going to deal with your problems. If the possibility of failure were erased, what would you attempt to achieve?"[7]

We have already established how the college years are full of ups and downs, highs and lows, and it will be through these times

---

[6] http://blogs.longhollow.com/david/?p=5708
[7] John Maxwell, *Failing Forward* (Nashville, TN: Thomas Nelson, 2000).

that you can succeed and, other times, that you may fail. How you respond to your failure will determine the direction you will go. Forward motion is the key!

You will have classes that you drop or maybe even fail. You may or may not get in the sorority that you have always longed to be in, or that fraternity might reject you. Don't let the weight of finals week, recruitment week, pledging, friends, or bad breakups take you down. When you fail, it is okay—just get back up and keep going. Just don't fall back into the same failure and stay in that ditch—get up, dust yourself off, and move forward.

Those who fall back into the same failure are those who never reflect on their failures. Maybe this is what Paul was challenging us with when he covered the topic of being "dead to sin" in Romans 6:1–2: "What should we say then? Should we continue in sin so that grace may multiply? Absolutely not! How can we who died to sin still live in it?" Paul challenges us that just because God forgives us and picks us up from our failures does not mean we should keep failing in the same way over and over again. Let your failures propel you forward to become more like Christ every day, and always remember that God is still God regardless of the trial-and-error experiences we walk through in our lives.

## Take Ownership

When we fail, we must own up to our mistakes. We must own our errors. Leif Babin and Jocko Willink, in their book *Extreme Ownership*, made this statement:

> Every leader and every team at some point or time will fail and must confront that failure. Often our mistakes provided the greatest lessons, humbled us, and enabled us to grow and become better. For leaders, the humility to admit and own mistakes and develop a plan to overcome

them is essential to success. The best leaders are
not driven by ego or personal agendas. They are
simply focused on the mission and how best to
accomplish it."[8]

They then go on to challenge the concept of "extreme ownership." I would say one of the foundations of success in college is
learning to own your mistakes. You will never overcome and learn
from a mistake you have never owned up too. Life gives us trials
through success and failures, but it's our job to own up to the truth
from these life lessons.

## How to Take Ownership

1. Surround yourself with a godly community that
   you can share your trial and errors with and who
   will pray with and for you.
2. Find a godly mentor who can walk with you
   through these life lessons. A great place to find
   this person is in a local church.
3. Confession leads to health. Take time each day
   to confess and repent along with giving thanks.
4. Develop a discipline to spend time in God's Word
   daily.

All four of these things will help you take extreme ownership
in developing a healthy foundation in your life.

---

[8] Jocko Willink and Leif Babin, *Extreme Ownership: How U.S. Navy
SEALs Lead and Win* (New York: St. Martin's Press, 2015), 8.

## Chapter 16

# Greater Is He!

**AS WE DISCUSSED EARLY** in this book, it's through your moment of salvation that Christ comes to live within you through the power of the Holy Spirit. Our prayer is that if you are reading this book and you have never taken that first step of surrender that you would do that today. Without that first step, none of what we are hoping to equip you for will be possible. We've all sinned and fallen short of the glory of God. There is none of us righteous, not even one. For those of you reading this who have taken that step, Ephesians 1:13–14 says, "In him you also were sealed with the promised Holy Spirit when you heard the word of truth, the gospel of your salvation, and when you believed. The Holy Spirit is the down payment of our inheritance, until the redemption of the possession, to the praise of his glory." At your point of salvation the same Spirit that raised Christ from the dead comes to live within you! You are chosen, you are adopted into His family, you are heirs, and you are His!

Through your newfound identity in Christ, you can boldly declare this truth that the enemy can't. Remember, Satan is our enemy, or as Jesus refers to him in John 10:10, the thief: "A thief comes only to steal and kill and destroy. I have come so that they may have life and have it in abundance." Never forget the reality that you do have a real enemy who wants nothing more than to steal from you, to kill you, and ultimately take you out and destroy you. The pitfalls of the college experience are exactly and intentionally his ploy and tactical means to do just that. He will go to great lengths to trip you up and take you out!

First Peter 5:8 refers to our enemy as a "roaring lion, looking for someone to devour" (NIV). But verse 9 says, "Resist him, standing firm in your faith." I share these verses with you to make you aware that not only do you have a very real enemy who knows you, but he knows your weaknesses, he knows how to try and trip you up, he studies you just like an opponent in sports watches game film. One of the purposes that an athlete watches game film is to study the opponent's weakness and then to expose those weaknesses in the game. When the enemy "seeks" after you, he is trying to expose you through your weaknesses.

To live a different college experience, you must understand where you are weak, accept it, and grow through it. Otherwise the enemy will win, over and over again, in your life. I had a young man meet with me who confessed to a heavy pornography addiction that he had struggled with for years. He said, "The enemy is winning against me when it comes to pornography." As we talked, I asked him if he had removed the app in which he is downloading porn; his response was "no." He had done nothing with the area where he was the weakest, so he left the door open, exposing himself and being completely vulnerable for the enemy to win, time and time again in his life in this area of weakness.

In order to live a different college experience, we must recognize where we are weak and change! This sometimes feels as if it is an impossible task.

But here is the exciting news today . . . *greater* is He!

I love the promise we have in 1 John 4:4: "You are from God, little children, and you have conquered them, because *the one that is in you is GREATER than the one who is in the world*" (emphasis mine). We know the enemy so desires to win against us and he is crafty in his work. He knows where we are weak and wants to expose us.

Yet, there is a strong truth for those who have surrendered their life over to Jesus Christ as their Lord and Savior. And that truth is that "Greater is He!"

> Greater is He, than your weakness.
>
> Greater is He, than your sin.
>
> Greater is He, than our Enemy.
>
> Greater is He, than any temptation you will come up against.
>
> Greater is He, than your past.
>
> Greater is He!

This passage is not a passage just to be declared lightly. This is a promise to not just claim but stand on in your walk with the Lord throughout your life. When John was writing this passage in 1 John 4, he was referring back to the false prophets of that day to remind believers to know that our God is greater than any other god. Greater is He! We can stand on passages like 1 Corinthians 10:13: "No temptation has overtaken you except what is common to mankind. And God is faithful; he will not let you be tempted beyond what you can bear. But when you are tempted, he will also provide a way out so that you can endure it" (NIV), because we know that greater is He that is in me, than he that is in the world (1 John 4:4). We can walk through the world of temptation, valleys of heartache, struggles with identity, and so much more by simply resting on this fact: *I will never face more than the One who is in me can bear.*

Greater is HE!

Through the course of this book, we have covered fifteen different topics to help empower you to live out a different college experience. But what good is the challenge to live differently over these next few years in college if you don't even believe that you can? I have met many college students and young adults who say they want to change, but that they just can't. So many have tried to give up pornography, overcome bulimia, find freedom from anxiety or loneliness, sober up from drunkenness, or overcome their sexual sin, and they have failed to do so because they just can't do it.

I for one can identify with them—*we* can't. *We* can't do it on our own. But that's just the thing . . . on your own efforts, it will be impossible for you to live a different college experience. Apart from the power of God working in and through your life, you can do nothing. The world has tried over and over again to fix what it can't. It is only through Jesus that we have the power to conquer the flesh and the sinfulness of our hearts. Jeremiah even understood how wicked the heart is. He said in Jeremiah 17:9, "The heart is deceitful above all things and beyond cure" (NIV). No one has ever come up with a cure for the issues of the heart except for Jesus! Through the death and resurrection of Jesus Christ, He paid the price for our sins. Through Jesus Christ, we are made righteous. It is through Him alone—not based on anyone or anything else!

When we encounter the mountains of life, all we tend to see is the mountain in front of us that we cannot climb. We view the circumstances of life and often times we live defeated. Those that go into a game thinking they will lose will lose every time. We must wake up each day knowing our heart is deceitful and, yes, the enemy is after us, but greater is He that is in us than he that is in this world. Our God is greater! That is John's message against the false prophets of his day, and that's the message to us today.

Our God is greater!

Through this life you might have faced some losses, some defeats. You might even feel as if there is no hope for you. I meet with a lot of college students who tell me that they have gone so far off that it just did not matter anymore. It was the hopeless lies that they believed about themselves that left them living in defeat, and so they chose to live out of that defeated belief instead of choosing to rise above it. So many of them try to end our conversation by saying, "It just is what it is."

But I don't believe that. Never accept defeat! Let me encourage you today from James 4:7–8, "Therefore, submit to God. Resist the devil, and he will flee from you. Draw near to God, and he will draw near to you. Cleanse your hands, sinners, and purify your hearts, you double-minded." Submit yourself to God and run from your past, or even your present, and pursue God with your future. You can resist the devil and his evil schemes because greater is He! The Holy Spirit within you is more powerful than the forces of deception, hopelessness, and blindness that are against you.

As we wrap up this book on how you can live a different college experience, I want us to close by looking at the best example that there is for us to model our life after—the life of Jesus Christ Himself. In both Matthew 4:1–11 and Luke 4:1–13, you will find the accounts of the temptation of Jesus. In both of these passages, immediately following His baptism by John the Baptist, we find Jesus "full of the Holy Spirit." He was then "led by the Spirit" into the Judean wilderness where He was tempted by the devil over a period of forty days. Over the course of these forty days He fasted from food on top of the temptations of the devil. Yet it is in this "desert season" that we see part of God's greater plan for Jesus' life here on earth to prepare Him for the ministry and mission that He came to accomplish. This was a time in Jesus' life of clarity and refining, and we see that God the Father was with Him through this journey—He was never alone.

Three times in these passages Satan tempts Him with different things, but it's His response that is where the power is! Notice that each time He responds to the temptation by quoting Scripture: "It is written . . ." I think there is so much in this encounter between Jesus and His temptations from Satan that we can glean, as well as when it comes to overcoming and truly living a "greater is He" life. The provision in the wilderness that Jesus clung to and His ammunition to combat the lies and temptations from His enemy was the Word of God. Jesus Himself used the Word of God to combat the temptations of His enemy. This is why it's imperative that we, too, know the Word of God—so that when we are tempted we can combat the lies of the enemy with the Word of Truth. You see, Satan knew Jesus' purpose here on earth was to redeem us and make right all that had been broken by sin in the garden in Genesis 3. And he tried everything in his power to derail Jesus' mission and trip Him up.

But this time was different. Unlike the first time we read about the serpent in the Garden of Eden who deceived Adam and Eve by his cunning and craftiness, Jesus knew His enemy and knew his tactics and knew that He was greater! These forty days in the wilderness when Jesus overcame these temptations of the enemy prepared Him for the endurance He needed to persevere to the very end of the battle, to win the ultimate victory of why He came to this earth, and that was to endure the cross and glorify Himself through His resurrection. Greater is He!

If we will allow Jesus' example in these passages to shape us and equip us for our journey ahead, we, too, will find that it's through His strength that we can have the endurance we need to be found faithful with this life that we've been given. It's through the Word of God that we, too, can be equipped for what God has called us to do and equipped to stand firm against the schemes of the enemy! Always remember, it's never going to be possible for you to live a different college experience apart from the power of God working in and through your life. But it is possible *with* God! That is what is so powerful about living a different college experience. So believe it! Go for it! And enter this new season of your life more confident than ever in who you are and Who is on your side, because greater is He!

To live a different college experience, let your life declare, "Greater is He!"

# Conclusion

The University of Alabama is best known for two things: championship football and a pervasive Greek life. At the start of my freshman year in 2014, I arrived on the UA campus as a sixth-generation ATO legacy. With that came some pressure and expectations to join the leviathan that is UA Greek life. However, instead of rushing a fraternity, I accepted a scholarship opportunity and became a member of the Blount Undergraduate Initiative, a liberal arts program/minor that had its own classes, professors, and dorm.

I had been to church my whole life up until this point. I presented a thesis on predestination versus free will, gave the talk on a Wednesday night at youth group, and was junior class president and student body president at my private Christian high school. Like many high school kids in the South, I was a regular church attendee and also was a believer that I had to earn my way into heaven. However, like many other high school kids in the South, I also led a separate, shameful life of sin that was hidden from the eyes of my friends and family.

Now we are back to freshman year, but near the end of the first semester. I had yet to succumb to the temptations of alcohol or drugs, but I was just as dead inside as someone who had fallen to these sins. I can count on one hand the amount of times I had been to church as well as the number of Christians I had pouring into me. I was exhausted at this point; I felt like every conversation I had I was defending my faith to several people within my program that were much smarter than me. However, that semester I made one of the most important decisions of my life, I joined a freshman guy's small group that changed my life forever.

After finishing my small group freshman year, I became a small group leader at that same church the next year. That freshman small group was the first time I ever heard someone else open up about the private sexual sins that they struggled with. This was groundbreaking for me, and the Lord used it to change my heart toward vulnerability and accountability. Throughout my sophomore year, I was learning more about God's grace and Jesus' sacrifice, but I was still trying to earn that grace and love.

My junior year I became a Young Life leader at Tuscaloosa Academy. When I became a Young Life leader, the Lord began to open my eyes to the gospel at its most basic form, as I was having to present it in this form to kids who had never really heard it before and I no longer had the opportunity to hide behind layers of theology. God used my junior year to show me that no matter what I did, I couldn't make Him love me any more or any less.

Now, as a college senior, I can reflect and see a few clear points where the Lord has clearly changed my life. First was when I was a freshman and He showed me what true community looked like. Without the encouragement and honest accountability from my brothers in Christ my freshman year, I would not be the man that I am today. Second, was when I was a LifeGroup leader my sophomore year. This is when the Lord started to pull me alongside Him by showing me how to start working toward spiritual discipline in the form of spending time alone with Him and by loving people in my small group who were different from me in almost every way imaginable. And in my last two years of college the Lord has pruned and reshaped my life by radically changing my view of Him. Instead of striving to earn His affection and approval, He showed me that those things are freely given to me; all I have to do is set aside my pride and accept them.

—Matthew McDavid, Young Life leader at Tuscaloosa Academy; senior, University of Alabama

Don't let college get the best of you; get the best out of it. God has opened the door for you to be at the school He wants you to be at in this season of your life. Go and thrive. Grow to become the man or woman that God intends for you to be, not what the world pushes you to be. You get to make that choice, and I pray this book has helped you to choose the right and the wise path for your college experience, based on the Word of God and your pursuit to become more like Him.